HISTORY

OF THE

First Reg't Pennsylvania Reserve Cavalry,

FROM

ITS ORGANIZATION, AUGUST, 1861,

TO

SEPTEMBER, 1864,

WITH

LIST OF NAMES OF ALL OFFICERS AND ENLISTED MEN

WHO HAVE EVER BELONGED TO THE REGIMENT, AND REMARKS ATTACHED TO EACH NAME, NOTING CHANGE, &c.

COLONELS:

GENERAL GEORGE D. BAYARD,
From August, 1861, to May, 1862.

HON. OWEN JONES,
From May, 1862, to January, 1863.

COL. JOHN P. TAYLOR,
Since January, 1863

PHILADELPHIA:
KING & BAIRD, PRINTERS, No. 607 SANSOM STREET.
1864.

PREFACE.

Headquarters, Camp, First Pennsylvania Reserve Cavalry,
SEPTEMBER 9th, 1864.

To the Officers and Enlisted Men of the First Pennsylvania Reserve Cavalry.

GENTLEMEN :—Knowing the deep interest felt in the history of the regiment, by every member who has shared its services, its dangers and hardships, and is thereby entitled to a portion of its well-earned merits, I have endeavored to collect the prominent incidents of its operations; and during the comparative leisure of the last month have arranged them in a condensed form for publication, that all who wish might be supplied with a copy.

You will find the following pages to contain a sketch of the organizing, arming and equipping of the regiment, a summary of its services from the time it entered the field to the present date, with brief descriptions of the part it took in the various actions in which it was engaged, a tabular statement of name and date of each battle and skirmish, date, route and distance of each march and scout, with general remarks, &c. Also, the name, rank and date of commission, of each officer, the name and rank of each enlisted man, (the latter arranged in companies, and each company prefaced by a short sketch of its organization,) with remarks also appended to the names of both officers and men, noting all changes that have taken place.

The object, however, in preparing this work, was not to write a history of the regiment, nor to enter into a minute or detailed account of its operations, but simply to furnish a brief summary of its services, with any other data that might be interesting to its members. Neither is it supposed that the hasty and condensed narrations, these pages contain, will elicit any interest from the public at large, as they are strictly local in their character; but, if they meet your approval, it will be answering my fullest expectations. You will, doubtlessly, discover in their perusal, numerous omissions and inaccuracies, as many of the incidents, especially of the first year, have been sketched from memory, and the numerous and constant changes incident to a regiment in the field, renders it very difficult to furnish correct data in every instance; but, conscious that you are aware of the disadvantages labored under in the preparation of a work of this kind, here in active service, where our respites from duty are so brief and irregular, I therefore respecfully submit it to your consideration, trusting that though it may not reach what you would desire it to be, its contents, may, at least, not be devoid of interest.

Very respectfully, your obedient servant,

WM. P. LLOYD,

Adjutant First Penna. Reserve Cavalry.

INTRODUCTION.

STRANGERS to war, and especially to the blighting curse of intestinal and fratricidal strife, the year of 1861, as it opened upon our happy and prosperous nation, with events so new and startling and portentuous of coming evil, found the public mind resting in the quiet calm of its accustomed security. True, for some months previous, the murmur of discord and dissatisfaction, with an occasional bold and daring threat or menacing overt act, from the southern half of the nation, betokened a determination of purpose, more serious and alarming than had, at any previous period of our history, marked the wrangling of parties and the clashing of sectional interests.

But, the stormy season of a Presidential campaign had just passed, and the majority of the people, at least in the North, expected, as always has been the case heretofore, that after the conflicting elements had spent their fury, and the efforts of the partizan leaders, either crowned by victory or subdued by defeat, the public mind would subside into its usual quiet and decorum. Still, there were some, who, marking the course of events for years, saw, in the unusual signs of the times, foreshadowings of the storm that was soon to burst on our devoted land.

As day after day of the new year passed, events stranger and more startling were developed, and thus matters continued growing more desperate until the fourth of March, when a new Chief Executive was inaugurated and the reins of Government passed into the hands of another Administration ; but, instead of these events having any effect in allaying the angry and discordant elements, the storm-cloud of civil commotion grew rapidly darker and more threatening.

The warlike preparations of the South now too began to arouse the loyal people of the nation to the stern fact that treason, real earnest treason, was rapidly spreading its contaminating bane over large tracts of the nation's territory, rife for any deed, and ready in its daring audacity to attempt any crime, and that rebellion in gigantic proportion was upon them.

All who lived through those days of intense excitement, from March to the middle of April, when the traitor's cannon first defiled our nation's ensign as it floated over the wall of Sumter, remember, and will doubtlessly cherish, while memory retains vitality to perform her offices, the anxiety which wrapped every loyal heart in a murky pall, during those hours of painful suspense, when the nation hung vibrating between war, just and honorable, as we are now prosecuting it, and ignominious peace with anarchy, or at best—traitor's rule. Long, too, will be remembered the days of almost frantic excitement that followed the dishonoring of our flag at Charleston. How, as with one giant throb of the nation's great heart, her loyal sons arose, and from workshop, from store, from farm, from the nursery of learning, the lawyer's office and the minister's sacred desk, men of every avocation, circumstance and calling, rushed forward to vindicate its insulted dignity.

The first call for seventy-five thousand men, being immediately filled, thousands who applied were unable to get into the service. These, forming in companies throughout the country, remained to await subsequent events.

During this time the material of the FIRST PENNSYLVANIA RESERVÈ CAVALRY was principally collected, as was also the balance of the Reserve Corps, most of which, however, had the advantage of some months drilling in camps of instruction in an organized condition, while this regiment remained scattered in parts of companies, over the State, few of them having an official existence.

The companies remained in this unorganized and scattered condition, until about the middle of July when a few of them assembled at Camp Curtin, and commenced the formation of a regiment.

ORGANIZATION.

(Notes of Organization furnished by Surgeon G. B. HOTCHKIN.)

"THE First Cavalry regiment of Pennsylvania Reserve Volunteer Corps was organized at Harrisburg, Pennsylvania, August, 1861, by His Excellency, Governor Andrew G. Curtin, under the provisions of a special law authorizing the Governor to raise, arm and equip a force consisting of twelve regiments of infantry, one rifle, one artillery and one cavalry regiment. This was to be a State force under the control of the Governor, to be held in readiness to meet any emergencies that might arise from the events of the war.

"The defeat of General McDowell, at Bull Run, July 21st, 1861, occasioned just such an emergency before the organization was complete. Five companies of cavalry, which were then in Camp Curtin, were immediately organized by the election of Captain Hastings, U. S. A., as Colonel, and Captain Owen Jones, as Major, and the battalion sent to Washington, with the rest of the Reserve Corps, where they were soon joined by two additional companies from Harrisburg."

"The removal of the regiment from the State before it was completely organized, equipped and trained for service, as contemplated by the law of its organization, caused much feeling of disappointment in the State, and the officer selected for the command of the regiment, declined to go with it in its unorganized condition.

"The seven companies remained in camp near Washington, about a month, with a deficiency of organization, which threatened total failure of the attempt to form a regiment.

"The field and company officers present, being little schooled in military tactics and discipline, though quite anxious to become soldiers and to make their men such, fully realized their deficiencies, and anxiously sought for assistance."

"Through the influence and advice of General Stoneman, then Chief of Cavalry, in conjunction with the Governor of Pennsylvania and his advisers, the service of Lieutenant George D. Bayard, was secured as Colonel, and he assumed command of the regiment about the first of September, 1861, and immediately commenced drilling, and fitting it for active service.

"About this time, also, three companies from a disbanded regiment were attached to this command, and its organization completed, by the election of of Captain Jacob Higgins, to the post of Lieutenant-Colonel, and the appointment of S. D. Barrows as Adjutant, and Lieutenant R. R. Corson, Regimental-Quartermaster."

The regiment then consisted of Companies A, Captain Robison; B, Captain Stadelman; C, Captain Taylor; D, Captain Gile; E, Captain Wolf; F, Captain Harper; G, Captain Gardner; H, Captain J. B. Davidson; I, Captain McNulty, and K, Captain Boyce.

"The appointment of Surgeon David Stanton, Assistant Surgeon, Samuel Alexander and Chaplain J. Hervey Beale, shortly after, completed the regimental staff."

"January, the seventh, 1862, two independent companies, Company L, Captain Hoffeditz, and Company M, Captain Richards, were attached to the regiment, thus making it a complete regiment of twelve companies.

"The regiment was originally armed by the United States Government, with sabre and pistol to each man, and ten carbines to each company, the number of carbines having been increased at different times, until the whole regiment was ultimately supplied with them, in September, 1862.

"The greater part of the original horses of the regiment were selected with great care, and purchased by some of our own officers in the State of Pennsylvania; the remainder were selected by Colonel Bayard himself, from the Government horses at Washington. These horses, under good care and training during the succeeding winter became notably the best regiment of horses in the United States, and some of them remain still the best horses, after a half dozen new lots have been worn out in the service of the regiment."

"The material of this regiment was choice in its character, the Governor refusing all applications for the formation of companies for the regiment, from large towns and cities, it was gathered from various sections of a great State, at a time when infantry was the favorite arm of service. The men who joined this regiment, chose the service for the love of it, and because they were horsemen. They were mostly country laborers and farmers, accustomed to the use and care of horses, and at least good, if not properly trained riders. Very few of our men were dismounted by accident or awkwardness during their drilling, or since then, in the service they have performed. Most of them were accustomed to labor and fatigue, and well calculated to endure the hardships incident to a cavalryman in the field. A few old soldiers, among both officers and men, contributed much more than their personal labor toward the proper training of the regiment.

"The greatest defect in material seems to have arisen, either from want of proper examination of recruits, or want of knowledge of the requirements of cavalry service, on the part of examining surgeons. This has been a fruitful cause of discharges for disability in our regiment, but most of our deficient men would have been fully able to do infantry service, although from various causes unable to endure service in the saddle."

"After Colonel Bayard was established in his position, and his regiment armed, equipped and mounted, the work of drilling was immediately commenced, and prosecuted with all the energy for which that officer was so much noted. This was not done after the usual manner of drilling cavalry by a course of gradual training, but the attempt was made to bring the regiment to the most effective condition for actual contact with the enemy, in the shortest possible time, as the cavalry arm of the service must be *made* and not improved merely. To this end the officers were called to meet the Colonel, once or twice daily, to study tactics, and the fear of the Examining Board kept constantly before them to stimulate their energies to the utmost. Company, squadron and regimental drill and sabre exercise, on foot or mounted, were pushed to the utmost, morning and afternoon of every day, under the personal direction of Colonel Bayard and his field officers, while various scouts and daily picket duty, by detail, served to impress their lessons by actual practice of duty near the enemy."

WINTER QUARTERS AT PIERPONT.

We crossed the Potomac river, as the advance of General McCall's command, on the 10th day of October, 1861, and were stationed at Camp Pierpont, at the extreme right of the Army of the Potomac. Here we picketed by details of one officer, and thirty men, daily, during the winter, also, making frequent expeditions to Drainesville and toward Leesburg.

The first skirmish of the regiment, occurred near Drainesville, on the 27th day of November, 1861. The regiment, had been ordered out on the previous evening, to scout the country beyond Difficult creek, a small stream crossing the pike, about six miles west of camp, and make a descent on Drainesville, a village some seven miles further on.

Marching all night and arriving at the village just

before daylight, the houses were surrounded, and a search for guerrillas, reported to harbor there, commenced.

Half a dozen suspicious persons were arrested, and the regiment, after an hour's halt, took up its march for camp. When some two miles from the town, the head of the column was fired on by guerrillas concealed in the pine thickets, by the roadside. Detachments immediately dismounted and pushed into the woods, and in a few minutes had killed or captured the whole party of the enemy. We lost, Assistant Surgeon Samuel Alexander and private Jos. Hughling, Company D, killed, and two other men severely wounded. Colonel Bayard was slightly wounded and his horse killed under him.

BATTLE OF DRAINESVILLE.

Five companies, under Lieutenant-Colonel Jacob Higgins, participated actively in the battle of Drainesville, December 20th, 1861, and General Ord highly complimented Colonel Higgins for the valuable service the cavalry rendered during the action. At the opening of the engagement, the cavalry was ordered to push forward and compel the enemy to unmask his position This was done in gallant style by Lieutenant-Colonel Jacob Higgins, with H and I companies, dashing forward on the road, south of the town, while C, D and E companies charged directly through the town, and pushed on, until the enemy, opening on their flank and rear, compelled them to withdraw to prevent being cut off. The infantry now becoming engaged, the cavalry was ordered to the support of

Easton's battery, and remained drawn up in the rear of it, though subjected to a heavy artillery fire, until the close of the action, which lasted about one hour and twenty minutes, and ended in the total rout of the enemy

Here was the first time that any part of the regiment had been called upon to face the enemy in battle array, and its action on this occasion very truly reflected, or rather foreshadowed, its subsequent history.

The winter of '61 and '62 was spent at Langley, or Camp Pierpont, some four miles west of Chain Bridge, the regiment being engaged in the services before mentioned, until the 10th of March, when winter quarters were broken up and campaigning commenced.

OPENING OF SPRING CAMPAIGN OF 1862.

The regiment then marched with the Pennsylvania Reserve Corps, in the grand advance toward Manassas, and after about ten days most exhausting service, exposed to pelting rain, sleet and snow storms, returned to Falls Church, where we remained until General McDowell's advance toward the Rappahannock. Starting on the 9th of April, we marched *via* of Fairfax Court House and Manassas Junction to Catletts Station, which we reached on the 11th, and there performed scouting and picket duty, till the middle of the month.

On the 13th we started on a reconnoissance toward Falmouth, and having driven in the enemy's outposts and ascertained his situation, returned to camp.

On the 17th, two battalions of our regiment supported by a portion of the Second New York Cavalry, marched toward Falmouth, as the advance guard of General McDowell's army. That day we skirmished with the enemy's outpost, from Hartwood Church toward Falmouth and during the night were led into an ambuscade near the town, and after severe fighting were compelled to rest till daylight.

Having marched and skirmished all day and until a late hour of the night of the 17th, the men were permitted to take a few hours' sleep at the feet of their horses, and were again in the saddle, ready to move forward, at two o'clock, on the morning of the 18th.

Every precaution having been taken to prevent any noise in advancing that might warn the enemy of our approach, the column commenced its silent march toward the town, squadron L and M leading the advance.

The morning was cloudy, and so intensely dark, that the enemy's works, which consisted of a strong barricade, constructed of rails laid alternately lengthwise and crosswise, were not seen, until the advance guard was right on them. The column was thus brought to a halt, in a narrow road which it completely filled, and almost instantly a heavy fire of musketry was opened in the faces of the men.

The regiment recoiling before this fierce and unexpected attack, was immediately withdrawn from the road, and its operations directed against the flanks of the enemy's position, in a series of rapid and brilliant charges, which, however, were ineffectual in dislodging him, until daylight, when he fell back, and we occupied the town.

The history of this war will doubtlessly present, in all its records of daring, few parallels to this hazardous dash. A body of cavalry charging on a town, garrisoned by double its number of infantry, along an unknown road, and through the blinding darkness of a rayless night. We were not veterans then, neither were our generals.

In this action, Company E, commanded by Captain Marcus L. French; Company F, commanded by Captain Alexander Davidson; Company K, commanded by Captain J. H. Williams; Company L, commanded by Captain W. A. Sands, and Company M, commanded by Captain J. H. Richards, all under the charge of Lieutenant-Colonel Owen Jones were closely engaged. Companies G, H, and I, under Major R. J. Falls, acted as a reserve and were not engaged until the next morning.

Colonel Bayard, in an official report to the Governor of the State of Pennsylvania, complimented the regiment in the highest terms, for its conduct on the occasion.

The first day after the action the regiment encamped a short distance from Falmouth, and a few days afterward moved several miles down the neck, and commenced doing picket duty along the Rappahannock river, and scouting on the Peninsula below. While engaged in this we had frequent skirmishes with the enemy across the river, and on one occasion, when he attempted to recapture a schooner from the First New Jersey Cavalry, on the night of the 13th of May, Companies F, G, H, L, and M, turned out, and after a brief but sharp skirmish, drove him off, brought the schooner to our own shore of the river, and rescued the men on board, several of whom were wounded.

The following is a report of the affair, by Colonel Jones, Commanding Regiment.

Headquarters, First Pennsylvania Reserve Cavalry,
May 14th, 1863.

"General George D. Bayard.

"General:—I have the honor to report that on the evening of yesterday, May 13th, heavy firing was heard at my camp from the line of our pickets on the Rappahannock. I soon learned that it proceeded from a party of the enemy, and was directed at a vessel in charge of the First New Jersey Cavalry. I at once ordered the carbineers of my command to proceed to the river bank, and finding that the vessel was fastened to the north bank of river, and in charge of our pickets, I ordered my men to be placed in position to cover the removal of two men of the First New Jersey Cavalry, that were on board of her, and had been badly wounded by the fire of the enemy, giving orders not to fire, unless first fired upon. After the first, and just as the second man was being removed from the vessel, a heavy fire was opened upon her by the enemy, and was instantly replied to by a heavy and well sustained fire from my men, posted along the river bank. As soon as the enemy's fire ceased, the order to cease firing was given, and the remaining wounded men removed with safety.

"It gives me great pleasure to state that in the

effort, none of my men were hurt, and that the officers and men displayed the utmost promptitude bravery and coolness."

Colonel Bayard having received appointment as Brigadier-General, Lieutenant-Colonel Owen Jones was chosen Colonel, and took command of the regiment May 5th, 1862.

M'DOWELL'S ADVANCE MAY 25TH AND OPERATIONS IN THE SHENANDOAH VALLEY.

On the afternnon of the 25th of May, when General McDowell commenced his advance to join forces with General McClellan, the regiment crossed the Rappahannock at Fredericksburg, and was sent forward to find the enemy. We advanced rapidly towards Richmond, and reached a point on the Pamunky river, within fifteen miles of General McClellan's right wing on the evening of the 27th. The enemy falling back before us, and the whole route showing evidence of his hasty retreat. At this juncture, when all were jubilant over the prospects of soon joining the grand army of the Peninsula, against the Rebel Capitol, we received orders to return immediately to Fredericksburg. Recrossed the Rappahannock at that place on the evening of the 28th, and marched at once, *via* of Catlett's Station and Thoroughfare Gap to Front Royal, which we reached on the 1st day of June.

With but an hour's rest, we proceeded at full gallop, nearly to Strasburg, a distance of about twelve miles, when crossing the Shenandoah river and coming up to Jackson's forces, we skirmished until dark, and then recrossed the river and bivouacked for the night to await assistance next morning. General McDowell not having come up with his army our brigade, consisting of one battalion of Bucktails, Hall's Second Maine Battery, of three guns, the First New Jersey Cavalry, and First Pennsylvania Reserve Cavalry, proceeded alone, and driving Jackson's rear guard out of Strasburg, were almost immediately joined by the advance of General Fremont's army, entering from another direction.

A gallop of six miles, brought us upon the enemy's batteries at Woodstock, and after three repeated attacks, we drove them from their position, and his rear guard, consisting of infantry and cavalry, from the town.

In this manner, we proceeded for eight days under the guns of the enemy every day, and driving him as rapidly as General Fremont could follow with our main force.

At Mount Jackson, on the 4th, a running fight for the bridge across the Shenandoah, occurred, but the enemy reaching the river first, succeeded in crossing his forces, and destroying the bridge, thus delaying our column until the next day.

On the afternonn of the 6th, a sharp action occurred, just beyond Harrisonburg, in which the First New Jersey Cavalry, first, and later the Bucktail Battalion and our own regiment engaged a force of the enemy at least three times their number, and completely repulsed them.

On the 8th, we advanced and participated in the Battle of Cross Keys, but being the reserve, were but slightly engaged.

Next day we led the advance of the centre column to Port Republic, where we arrived just in time to witness the bridge, across the Shenandoah in flames and the enemy all safely beyond our reach.

On the 10th, we commenced retracing our steps down the valley, and, after a halt of two days at Mount Jackson, returned *via* of Front Royal again to Manassas, which point we reached on the 23rd, making thirty days of incessant marching, skirmishing and fighting, having in that time, marched nearly four hundred miles, skirmishing the greater part of the way in the face of the enemy, and having been engaged in two battles, and ten or twelve considerable skirmishes.

Remaining at Manassas to refit, as the efficiency of the command was much reduced by its late severe service, the regiment was engaged for the next two weeks in picketing in the direction of the Rappahannock.

POPE'S ADVANCE TO THE RAPIDANN AND RETREAT TO WASHINGTON.

We next marched with the advance of Pope's army, first to Manassas Junction, on the 4th of July, and some two weeks afterward to Rappahannock river and Culpepper.

From this latter point, as a centre, we made various marches, during the remainder of the month to Madison Court House, towards Gordonsville, &c.; also doing heavy picket duty at the same time.

On the 1st of August, we advanced with the brigade

to the Rapidann river, where picket and scout followed each other in regular reliefs, and our horses were seldom unsaddled day or night, from that time until, as rear guard, we came to Alexandria, closely followed by the enemy's advance, to within a few miles of that city; a period of about five weeks, day and night on duty.

"The duty on the Rapidann was very heavy. Our little party, about twelve miles from the advance of the army, for eight days guarding all the crossings of the river for several miles at a low stage of water, and at the same time watching at all points inland for the enemy's approach from above and below; making constant scouts to watch the country around us, was severely tried and all its endurance tested to the utmost."

When Jackson finally advanced in force, his first attempt on crossing the river, was to take our whole party before we could reach assistance, as he was fully aware of our location and force.

On the night of August 7th, 1862, the enemy crossed at several places and made attempts in the darkness, to surprise and capture our pickets, but was so skilfully baffled in his undertaking as to succeed in capturing but two men. The outpost rallying upon the reserve, held the enemy in check till morning, when the regiment withdrew some three miles and another stand was made to cover the crossing of the brigade over the Robinson river. Here the enemy were again delayed by a skilful management of our forces, until our camps were cleared, and our wagon train removed a safe distance to the rear, when we slowly retired, although subject to a brisk fire of artillery, and pursued by a strong force of infantry and cavalry, supported, as we afterward learned, by Jackson's whole force.

General Bayard, by his skilful manœuvering, and by the good conduct of our men, baffled the enemy's advance in force so completely, that nearly the whole day was occupied in returning to Cedar Mountain, a distance of but seven or eight miles from the point of attack on the previous evening.

Here, as a prelude to the bloody battle of the next day, we formed, and by holding the position until General Banks' force arrived, and deployed in battle order, traced the memorable lines, and measured off the ground, where before another day was half spent, more than twenty thousand men met face to face in mortal combat. A cool and determined front was kept continually toward the enemy, and as squadron after squadron filed off to the rear, the next in succession opened its front to the attack, until the preceding one had again taken up position, thus slowly and stubbornly giving ground, inch by inch, as the weight of the enemy's overwhelming force pushed us back.

"For this masterly retreat, General Bayard and his command received public compliment and thanks from the commanding General on the field next day."

BATTLE OF CEDAR MOUNTAIN.

The regiment was in front of the battle next day at Cedar Mountain as advance skirmishers, and the first battalion after skirmishing, was placed as support of Knapp's battery, which was making sad havoc with the enemy. A charge of a full division upon this battery placed it in imminent peril. A charge of cavalry was ordered. The first battalion dashed upon the enemy, broke three successive lines of infantry, turned and fought back; and of one hundred and sixteen men who started, about seventy-five formed their line again by the side of the battery. The advance of the enemy was completely checked by this daring charge, and the battery saved.

See subjoined extract of official report of MAJOR R. J. FALLS, *First Penna. Res. Cavalry.*

"IN THE FIELD, AUGUST 13th, 1862.

"SIR: According to your instructions, I beg leave to offer the following report of a charge, made by the first battalion of your regiment, under my immediate command, at the battle of Cedar Mountain, on the 9th instant, at about 5 o'clock P. M.

"I was directed by Brigadier-General Bayard to charge through the enemy's lines, at a point where they were supposed to be forming for a charge on our batteries.

"My command consisting of Companies A, B, C, and D, Companies A and B forming the first squadron, commanded by Captain Wm. Litzenberg of B company; and companies C and D, composing the second squadron, commanded by Captain J. P. Taylor of C company. Company A of the first squadron, being commanded for the time being by First Lieutenant Wm. T. McEwen of C company, and Lieutenant Kelly. Captain T. J. Frow being absent sick, and First Lieutenant Wm. H. Patterson having been detached as Aid to General Bayard, during the early part of the engagement. Company B was commanded by Second Lieutenant R. S. Lawsha, Captain Litzenberg being in command of the squadron, and First Lieutenant Wm. Buzby absent sick. Company C, of the second squadron, was commanded by Second Lieutenant R. J. McNitt, Captain Taylor being in command of a squadron, and Lieutenant Wm. McEwen detached in command of company A. Company D was commanded by Captain H. A. McDonald, First Lieutenant W. L. Holbrook and Second Lieutenant Wm. F. Butcher, until the former was severely wounded and the latter killed, when the command devolved entirely on Lieutenant Holbrook.

"After getting in front of the point designated, and being in column of fours, I immediately formed squadron, my command being already under fire.

"I moved forward at a rapid gait until within fifty yards of the enemy's lines, which I found in great force, and three in number, when I gave the command "charge," when, with loud and terrific cheering, my command charged through their lines, cutting, running down and scattering them in every direction, causing sad havoc and discomfiture in their ranks, as prisoners taken testify.

"After charging back and reforming I found my command reduced from one hundred and sixty-four, rank and file, to that of seventy-one, the remainder having been killed, wounded, or otherwise placed *hors du combat*, by their horses falling over those killed and wounded.

"Our little band there proving themselves true sons of the old Keystone state."

The third battalion, commanded by Lieutenant-Colonel S. D. Barrows, after the battle had fairly opened, was withdrawn from the skirmish line, and stationed immediately in rear of the centre, where it remained until ordered to withdraw at dark.

The second battalion occupied a position on the extreme right of our line of battle, as flankers and at one stage of the action was entirely cut off by a force of the enemy, but succeeded in eluding the trap prepared for it by remaining in its position until dark, and then coming in, under cover of the night.

Additional Particulars.—The fatigue of the previous twenty-four hours' unremitting and exhausting service, with the heat of an August sun and the clouds of dust the arid winds stirred from the parched earth, had well nigh overcome the men, so that when, as the sun's last rays vanished from the west, the enemy withdrew his pressing columns, they sank down at their horses feet, rein in hand, and were soon lost to surrounding dangers and the demands of supperless stomachs, in the unconscious embrace of that sweet restorer exhausted nature so much needed.

But the fleet hours of the brief night passed before the tired soldier had half finished his grateful repose. Morning dawned calm and beautiful, and opening day, as its approach was heralded by the golden streams that flooded the eastern horizon, appeared, as though conscious of the awful scene about to be enacted, to draw the rising mists as a veil of sorrow around its opening splendors, and shed a sombre hue over the face of nature.

The first streaks of morning light was the signal for the soldier to shake off his slumbers, and prepare for the coming conflict. A cracker, with a cup of coffee hastily prepared from the muddy water of a brook hard by, made our breakfast, and we were ready. During the night the infantry and artillery had taken their respective positions, and the cavalry, stretching along from right to left, a few hundred yards to the front, forming the advance skirmish line.

And thus we stood from early morning, hour after hour, in painful suspense, awaiting the opening gun, Eleven o'clock came, and still all was quiet, and the first keen anxiety having worn off, expressions of impatience could be heard passing along the ranks, as fretted by the wearying suspense, the feeling naturally arises in the human breast to dare the worst, rather than wear longer the galling chain.

But the scene was soon to be varied. A few moments after eleven, Generals Crawford, Banks and Bayard with their staffs, riding forward to reconnoitre, were opened upon by a battery, and our gunners immediately replied, and a sharp artillery duel ensued, which was continued with great vigor for nearly an hour, on both sides, but no infantry became engaged.

At 12 M., the firing had ceased and silence again reigned until half past three, when a lone gun from a battery of the enemy, on the point of Cedar Mountain again sounded forth the signal.

Another and another immediately answered it along the line, until, in a few minutes, the woods rang and the hills echoed with the storm of thunder that burst from a dozen batteries; soon the infantry, too, opened, and by four o'clock the battle raged with fury. A fiercer or more deadly contest, between the same number, is seldom directed by the god of war. A little more than seven thousand Union troops fought, and gallantly held in check, from three and a half P. M. until darkness ended the carnage, more than eight thousand rebels.

From four o'clock until seven, the battle raged with unabated fierceness, peal on peal rung out the cannon's thunder, growing louder and more intense every moment, while crash answered crash in the long unbroken roll of musketry, and never did her sons bear more nobly the starry emblem of our nation's glory, than during these wearisome and awful hours on the bloody plains around Cedar Mountain.

"After the battle of Cedar Mountain, our regiment was accorded the post of honor in the extreme advance, and remained there, when our men were actually shot in camp by the enemy's pickets, for about a week."

When Pope retired, on the 19th of August, General Bayard's command, increased to five regiments, formed the rear guard. Moving slowly back we passed through Culpepper at ten o'clock at night, and reaching Brandy station at midnight, rested until morning. At daylight our outposts were attacked by the enemy. Supporting them strongly and gradually falling back, we kept him at a respectful distance until we neared the Rappahannock, when gathering his forces for a final attack, with the view of turning our flank, and cutting us off from the river, he made a dashing charge, first on the second New York cavalry, which, struck while forming, was broken, and next on the first New Jersey cavalry which shared the same fate, by the second New York, which was in their immediate front, riding through and confusing its ranks.

This occurred in a strip of woods that skirted an open, cleared country, which extended in a semicircle of half a mile from the ford, and the First Pennsylvania Reserve Cavalry, which had passed on, and just emerged from the woods as the attack was made, drew up in line, one half in the open field, facing the woods and the other on one side, partially concealed by it.

On came the Johnnies, after breaking the line in the woods, yelling and whooping, and doubtlessly supposing they would have it all their own way, but they were shortly led to think otherwise. As soon as they had emerged from the woods, the First Pennsylvania moved on them from the front and at the same time swept around an unlooked-for column on the flank. This brought them very quickly to a stand and about the time they were preparing to take the back track, the two regiments in the woods which had in the mean time rallied, came thundering down on their rear, completing their route, and scattering them in every direction. Remaining in battle line for some time and no enemy making his appearance, we crossed the river.

On the 21st, we again joined Generals McDowell and Siegel's forces, and did picket duty, and participated in the skirmishes along the Rappahannock, from Rappahannock Station to Sulphur Springs, until we retired with General Siegel to Gainesville on the evening of the 27th, having been on constant duty and under fire every day.

Immediately on crossing the river, Company E, Captain M. L. French; Company F, Captain A. Davidson; Company G, Captain D. Gardner, and Company H, Captain Theodore Streck, the whole under charge of Major J. H. Ray were detached from the regiment and sent to Beverly Ford, on picket.

The next day, the 22nd, having been relieved by a body of infantry and a battery of artillery, the battalion retired a short distance from the river to rest and graze their horses, and just when some of the men had unsaddled and were grooming their horses, others absent hunting forage, and the detachment scattered generally, the enemy opened a battery of six guns on the point and at the same time charged across the river with a body of cavalry. But, although taken at this great disadvantage, those who were present immediately rallied, forming line and holding the enemy back, until the balance of the command had all got together, when it withdrew without the loss of a man or horse.

From this place the battalion was ordered on special duty at General Pope's headquarters and continued thus employed until after the battle of Bull Run, when it returned to the regiment.

On the 22nd day of August, also, a party of about a dozen men, in charge of Sergeant H. A. Wood, Regimental C. S. Sergeant, on their way from Catlett's Station to the regiment with rations, were waylaid and fired on by a squad of rebel infantry near Sulphur Springs, and at the same time closed in on from the rear by a squadron of cavalry and compelled to surrender. During the following night, however, Sergeant Wood succeeded in making his escape and joined the regiment next morning.

About the same time also, Jackson reached the rear of our army at Manasses Junction, cut off our supplies and the regiment was forced to subsist for the next ten days, on the scanty fare this desolate and wasted region afforded, which consisted principally of green corn, savored by an occasional emaciated sheep or pig. All who experienced the hardships of these, the most trying days the regiment had yet passed through, will remember the sleepless nights, after days of exhausting toil, and the commencement of another day's duty, without the preface of a breakfast or the prospect of a dinner, and as for our horses with their backs actually putrid from the constant pressure and wear of the saddles, which had not been permitted to be removed for weeks, fell down in the ranks from exhaustion and starvation, and were abandoned by the wayside. "This was headquarters in the saddle."

The night following the day that Jackson made his attack on Manasses, a portion of Stuart's cavalry, made a descent on Catlett's Station, where, with others, our division and regimental trains were parked, but by the energy and gallantry of Captain R. R. Corson, Division Quartermaster and Lieutenant George H. Baker, Regimental Quartermaster, who had collected the dismounted men and teamsters and barricaded the camp and prepared to resist an attack, and with the aid of Colonel Kane and a small party of Bucktails, who were encamped close by, succeeded in driving the raiders off before they accomplished any damage further than the destruction of half dozen of General Pope's headquarter teams.

BATTLE OF BULL RUN.

During the 28th day of August, we were acting as flankers and skirmishers to McDowell's army and received the enemy's first fire, near Gainesville. The next day attached to General Reynold's Division, we spent the whole day on the extreme left of the army, being under fire most of the time and occupied the same comparative position next day, till called on to form part of the column of cavalry, preparing for a grand charge. When the left wing of the army was forced back, we, with the other cavalry were detailed to arrest the stampede and were engaged in this until night-fall covered the bloody scenes of that ill-fated field.

With picket and skirmish daily, we, as part of the rear guard, closed up the remainder of that memorable retreat, and then with little more than one hundred horses and two hundred available men, commenced a new picket line outside of Washington.

EXTRACT FROM AN ACCOUNT OF THE BATTLE.

"The First Pennsylvania Reserve Cavalry claims the honor of drawing the first fire and of receiving the last, in the ever-memorable battle of the Second Bull Run. On the morning of the 28th day of August, 1862, one squadron, Companies I and M got between Jackson and Longstreet on the Thoroughfare Gap pike, and captured and brought out ninety-seven prisoners. The next morning Colonel Owen Jones made a reconnoissance toward Centreville, and was opened upon by a light battery of the enemy, this being the first shot fired on either side.

On the evening of the 30th, Sergeant (now First Lieutenant) F. S. Morgan with ten men held a road leading to Centreville until all the wounded were removed from the buildings in his rear. The rebels brought up a battery of four guns and attempted to drive the little squad, but without avail, until their task was completely accomplished, and this was the last fire of the engagement."

CAMP SOUTH OF WASHINGTON.

Establishing camp, September 1st, near Munson's Hill, on the outskirts of the defences of Washington, picketing the approaches of the city, where we remained some six weeks refitting for the field.

About the middle of September, five companies, G, H, I, K and L, under command of Major R. J. Falls, were sent to do duty with General Siegel at Centreville, and were employed in picketing the line of Bull Run and scouting the plains of Manassas.

On the 12th of October, a scout was made to Warrenton consisting of this detachment from our regiment, and one of about the same strength from the First New Jersey Cavalry, all under command of Lieutenant-Colonel Karze, (First New Jersey), which after a brief skirmish drove a body of the enemy's cavalry from the place, entered the town and captured and paroled upwards of fourteen hundred sick and wounded soldiers, who had been brought here by the enemy, from the battle-field of Bull Run.

On the 10th of October, the balance of the regiment in camp, led the advance and covered the return of the division in a four days' scout from Bailey's Cross Roads to the Rappahannock.

SECOND ADVANCE FROM THE POTOMAC OF 1862.

On the morning of the 27th day of October, in the face of the pelting torrents of rain and sweeping gusts of a fierce equinoctial, we again took up our line of march southward.

Our column consisted of some dozen regiments of cavalry, with the necessary train and transportation, and we consequently moved very slowly. More than half the day was spent before we were fairly on the road, and night came on before we had gotten a dozen miles from camp.

The next day we marched to the plains of Chantilly and establishing that place as a centre, immediately engaged in scouting the country beyond, as far as the Bull Run mountains on the west, and the Rappahannock on the south.

On the thirty-first with a force consisting of the First New Jersey, our own regiment and four pieces of artillery, we were attacked by an equal force of the enemy, at the village of Aldie, situated on the Middleburg and Upperville pike, and in a Gap of the Bull Run mountains. After a spirited action of some two hours, the enemy were repulsed and we remained master of the field.

On the 4th of November, we marched to join forces

with General McClellan's advance, which was moving southward from the Potomac, along the east side of the Blue Ridge. Halted for the night a short distance beyond Middleburg, and resuming march next morning, reached Upperville late in the afternoon; and, a few hours after, General Pleasanton had driven the enemy from the place.

Early on the morning of the 6th, we resumed the march, and after travelling a circuitous route of twenty miles, reached the Waterloo pike, some three miles southwest of Warrenton. Here we met the enemy, who immediately opened a battery on the head of our column.

Captain H. S. Thomas' squadron, companies L and M, was at once ordered forward as skirmishers, supported by companies I and K. Captain D. Gardner, with company G, was sent down the pike toward Waterloo, while Colonel Owen Jones, with the balance of the regiment, pushed across the country with the design of intercepting the enemy on the Sulphur Spring pike. But only waiting to give us a few shell, he limbered up before our guns could be gotten in position, and made off with such speed as to baffle all attempts to overtake him. Our artillery, however, paid its compliments to the support of his battery, (which consisted of about a regiment of cavalry,) in the shape of a shower of shot and shell, as they dashed over the hill in their endeavors to elude our cavalry.

After the pursuit was discontinued, and the different detachments had rejoined the command, we resumed the march, passing through Warrenton and halting for the night a few miles out on the Fayetteville road.

Next morning, the 7th, we started in a heavy snow storm for Fayetteville, and reaching it about noon, remained there until nearly dark, when we again moved forward in the direction of Rappahannock station. Arriving in the vicinity of the bridge, at nine P. M., Colonel Jones was ordered to charge the fording with the First Pennsylvania Reserve Cavalry, and save the bridge, if possible; which movement he accomplished with such skill and dash, as to completely surprise the enemy and drive him off before he could reach the bridge, or do any injury to it.

On the following morning we went into camp near the station and remained for twelve days, picketing the various fords above and below this point.

On the night of the 19th we were again in column of route, slowly plodding our way through mud and rain and intense darkness, toward Falmouth. After eight hours wearisome travel we reached Morrisville, seven miles distant, and halted until morning. Again on the road, we reached Hartwood church, drenched with rain and covered with mud; and the next day, after a wearisome march, made through mud knee-deep to our horses, we made Brook's station, and established camp.

Picketing and scouting in the direction of the Occoquan river and Dumfries, made up the duties of the regiment for the four weeks we remained here.

BATTLE OF FREDERICKSBURG.

At early dawn, on the morning of the 10th of December, we received orders to break camp and be ready to move at once; this was not done without some regret, as the men had already prepared neat and comfortable winter quarters.

The line of march was commenced an hour or two before night, in the direction of Falmouth. The roads being completely covered with ice, and darkness setting in it became very difficult to advance over the hilly and uneven road, and we soon halted for the night. In the saddles again at six the next morning and reached Falmouth about noon. Forming a mile to the rear of the town, we remained in that position until evening, when, retiring to a wood just in our rear, picketed our horses, and building huge fires, were soon bivouacked for the night, all except companies I and K, Captains J. M. Gaston and J. H. Williams, which were sent to the river at dark to cross on the lower pontoon, and picket on the other side between the enemy's outposts and the pontoon bridge.

The night was intensely cold, and little sleep was had by the regiment, but the morning dawned clear and beautiful on the heights, where, soon after daylight, we stood formed ready for the advance; though the river and the lowlands, which, at this place, skirt its banks on the north side for half a mile, and on the south for full a mile back from the water's edge, were shrouded in thick clouds of mist.

The regiment, with the brigade, reached the river bank about nine A. M., and in half an hour had passed over the pontoons and taken position on the hostile shore. Here we were joined by the squadron sent forward the night previous to picket, and the regiment having been detailed as advance skirmishers, with orders to proceed until we found the enemy, our line was at once formed, stretching for a mile across the plains, and the advance commenced.

We found the enemy about a mile from the river, just beyond the railroad, in force, and reported his position.

General Bayard having visited the front, ordered the regiment to fall back across the railroad; this movement was instantly followed by the enemy's skirmishers, and his battle line moving forward at the same time opened hotly upon us. Our carbineers replied coolly and rapidly, holding the position for fully an hour against these odds, and until the infantry skirmishers of the Pennsylvania Reserve Corps relieved us.

The next day we were again deployed as skirmishers, our line stretching across the field the entire breadth of our left wing, and through the dreadful length of that disastrous day, we were compelled to sit, a target for the enemy's artillery, (which poured from the adjacent heights a continuous stream of iron death on the plain below,) living an age in an hour, and every moment dragged out to an agonizing length by the oppressive suspense, produced by the grand and appalling surroundings, still the regiment remained where it had been placed, not a man swerving from his post, until the shades of night began to settle down upon that plain, now smoking with the warm life's blood of fifteen thousand Union soldiers, when we were relieved and withdrawn to the river bank.

DEATH OF GENERAL BAYARD.

About three o'clock in the afternoon of the 13th, when the storm of battle raged the fiercest, and flying shot and shell were crashing through our ranks and ploughing up the earth around us, the sad tidings of the fall of our beloved general reached us. It fell like a thunderbolt upon the regiment; men forgot themselves in danger in their anxious solicitude for their general, and plainly, for a while, could be discerned along that unwavering line of brave men, the stern and rigid lineaments battle stamps upon the features, softening into gentler lines beneath the melting influence of sympathy and sorrow, and then again growing doubly frigid and unrelenting, as revenge brought back to mind who dealt the murderous blow.

No one, among the many heroes who have fallen in this war, possessed more fully and unfeignedly the love and esteem of those whom he honored as their leader, than did General Bayard of his command, and especially of his own regiment the First Pennsylvania Reserve Cavalry.

To this brilliant and lamentable soldier and unsurpassed cavalry officer, the regiment owes the completeness of its organization, the rapidity of its training, the skill and steadiness of movement which have rendered it so successful in its manœuvers and evolutions in the face of the enemy, the careful training in picket duty, which have spared it the mortification of surprise, and enables it thus far, to exhibit a record in this respect few regiments can equal, and to his training and example the steadiness and quiet courage which rendered its actions so conspicuous on this bloody field, and drew from General Reynolds the highest encomiums as it stood unwavering under the whole weight of fire from Jackson's line, holding its position until relieved.

It is not unworthy of note here, that the First Pennsylvania Reserve Cavalry was the only cavalry regiment actively engaged in this ill-advised and sanguinary battle, the balance of the brigade, which crossed the river with us, having been massed under cover of the river bank, where it remained during the whole engagement.

EXTRACT OF REPORT OF COLONEL OWEN JONES, CONTAINING ADDITIONAL PARTICULARS OF OPERATIONS OF THE REGIMENT, FROM OCTOBER 27TH TO DECEMBER 14TH, 1862.

"As Colonel of the First Pennsylvania Reserve Cavalry, I have the honor to report to you the service performed by this regiment since the commencement of this present campaign:

"On the 27th of October, I left Bailey's cross roads, and marched to Chantilly, and a few days after was ordered with Bayard's brigade to report to General McClellan.

"On the 31st had a small skirmish with a cavalry force of the enemy, supported by a battery, at Aldie.

"On the 6th of November, companies L and M, Captains H. S. Thomas and Lieutenant H. S. Gaul being in advance, the brigade moving on Warrenton, were attacked by the Seventh Virginia Cavalry, with an artillery support. The engagement was short and decisive. The enemy were soon driven from their positions with loss of killed and captured.

"Immediately after I entered Warrenton with a portion of my regiment, and was shortly after joined by the other regiments connected with the Pennsylvania Reserves, and the remainder of General Bayard's brigade, in the afternoon of that day. During a violent snowstorm, I was ordered forward with two battalions of the regiment, and a section of artillery, to seize and save the bridge, at Rappahannock station. My cavalry cut off and captured the picket stationed at the north side of the river for the protection of the bridge. A regiment of infantry encamped on the opposite side, was shelled and driven from their camp, leaving behind them their tents and material, including the luggage and mess chests of the officers, which were subsequently taken possession of by my men. Thus successfully carrying out the objects of the expedition. I held the bridge for about forty-eight hours until relieved by a brigade of infantry.

"From that time until the 19th, the regiment was engaged in guarding the various fords above and below the bridge, during which time various detachments had several slight skirmishes with the enemy. On the evening of the 19th, the regiment moved for Brooks Station, where it arrived on the 22nd, and there remained until the 10th day of December, doing picket and scouting duty.

"Arrived opposite Fredericksburg on the 11th of December, early on the morning of the 12th, the regiment was ordered to take the advance of the brigade, crossed the Rappahannock where we were joined by two companies that had passed the river the evening previous to do picket duty.

"By order of General Bayard, the regiment was then deployed as skirmishers in front of the brigade, and advanced cautiously through a thick fog, meeting and driving before them the advance post of the enemy, and holding their position until relieved by the advance of the infantry. In doing this duty a very severe skirmish occurred, in which a number of men and horses were killed and wounded.

"The companies deployed as skimishers, were under the command of Captain William T. McEwen, M. L. French, H. C. Beamer, H. S. Thomas and Lieutenant H. S. Gaul.

"I cannot speak in too high terms of the officers and men engaged in this affair. All did their duty nobly. This regiment was the only one actually engaged in the fight of that day and bivouacked for the night on the field.

"The day following I was ordered with my regiment to report to General Reynolds, for duty, and by him was directed to watch the motions of the enemy on the left of the army during the entire day, exposed to a storm of shot and shell, seldom, if ever equalled. That duty was performed, and I have reason to believe, to the full and éntire satisfaction of the officers in command, no other cavalry being in that portion of the field.

"The men remained during the night in the position held by them during the battle : our loss having been heavy in horses, although, fortunately few of the men were hurt.

"The day following we were ordered to recross the river and picket the north bank of the Rappahannock for a distance of some ten miles below Fredericksburg, which duty is now being performed.

"It gives me great pleasure to be able to say that during the entire time, none of my men have been captured."

WINTER QUARTERS AT BELL PLAIN LANDING, VA.

The regiment continued thus employed until the 29th of December, when it moved to within a short distance of Bell Plain Landing, on the Potomac side of the neck and prepared winter quarters.

The industry and constructive genius of our men soon changed the appearance of a wooded hillside, the site for our camp, from a primeval forest, to a neat and comfortable village of seven or eight hundred soldiers. The place of tents was supplied by huts half dug in the hillside, with natural chimneys drilled through the bank on the upper side, and the portion of the hut above ground, finished by logs and clap boards made from lumber felled at the door.

These quarters were all the men wished, had they been permitted to enjoy them, but "the exigencies of the service" directed otherwise, and in little more than a month the regiment was moved to other ground about a mile distant, and its skill again tested, in constructing quarters. Here, fortunately, it was permitted to have a nominal home until we broke camp in April, but not to enjoy uninterruptedly its log-ribbed and mud-plastered palaces, as each alternate ten days during the whole winter was spent on picket along the Rappahannock, in the vicinity of King George Court House.

INCIDENTS OF THE WINTER.

On the 19th day of January, the regiment with the army, turned out to make another attempt at dislodging the enemy from his formidable position around Fredericksburg, by crossing the river at "United States Ford," some miles above that place, and assailing his flank. But a heavy rain storm setting in, the roads became impassable, the artillery and trains swamping in the mud, a few miles from their camps, and after three days splashing and floundering, the movement was abandoned and the troops drenched, bespattered and half frozen returned to their camps.

Shortly after this move, Colonel Owen Jones resigning, Lieutenant-Colonel J. P. Taylor was chosen Colonel of the regiment, and on the 10th of February following, Major D. Gardner, Lieutenant-Colonel.

While on picket at King George C. H., on the 17th of March a detachment consisting of Companies F, G, L and M, under command of Major McEwen, made a scout on the neck below, destroying a number of barges and boats employed in smuggling contraband goods across the Rappahannock.

Two nights after, another detachment, consisting of Companies I and K, under command of Major Gaston, was sent to West Moreland C. H. on a similar expedition. On arriving at Maddox creek, some ten miles below, the party was divided: Captain Williams with K company taking the road to Maddox creek landing, while Captain T. C. McGregor, with I company proceeded on toward the Court House, and returning by way of Leedstown, destroying a large boat and captured a smuggler's wagon, loaded with silks, shoes, fancy goods and imperial tea. All that could be carried was packed on the saddles, and the balance, with the wagon, was destroyed, and the party returned next day to headquarters, having more the appearance of a travellers' caravan, than a squadron of Yankee cavalry.

OPENING OF THE SPRING CAMPAIGN OF 1863.

At 9 A. M., April 12th, 1863, the "general," whose notes had not greeted our ears for several months, was again sounded. Tents struck and saddles packed, the regiment was soon on its way from Bell Plain landing, Va., toward the Rappahannock to do picket duty. Established picket headquarters near King George C. H. and picket the river from Falmouth to Port Conway. Continued at this duty until May the 9th, when it was relieved and marched to Potomac Creek bridge.

At Port Conway, the terminus of our line of picket along the river, a flanking chain of videttes extended across the country at right angles with the river, for some three miles; all below this was open and unguarded and occasional scouts were made in this region, to learn what was transpiring, waylay smugglers and destroy contraband goods. On Sunday, the 26th day of April, a scouting party started, under command of Lieutenant-Colonel Gardner, to go to Leedstown, on the Northern Neck, of Va. for the purpose of capturing some rebel soldiers, reported to be across the river visiting friends. The main body of the party left the lower picket lines about 4, A. M., and proceeded down on the Rappahannock road until they reached Leedstown

At 12.30 M. of the same day, Colonel Taylor, accompanied by an escort of one officer, (Lieutenant W. A. Kennedy, Company K,) and six men, proceeded in the direction the detachment had taken, for the purpose of intercepting it. When about eight miles below our line, they were fired upon by a large body of the Fifteenth Virginia (rebel) cavalry, dismounted and in ambush. Three of the number, Eli Leskelett, Moses Hastings, and Corporal David Ackelson, all from Company I, were riddled with bullets and fell from their horses dead, or mortally wounded. Colonel Taylor had his cap shot from his head and Lieutenant Kennedy his horse wounded, and both narrowly escaped being captured, by dashing through the guerrillas who thronged the road in front of them.

This cowardly crew was part of a detachment of about three hundred who had crossed the river in two large flat boats, after Colonel Gardner's party had passed down, with the intention of intercepting their return. Destroying the bridges and posting parties in ambush on the different roads, they would doubtlessly have succeeded in their dastardly designs of murdering more of our men, but for the alarm occasioned by the attack made on Colonel Taylor and his party, which was communicated to Colonel Gardner, by negroes who had witnessed the affair, thereby enabling him by skilful movements to evade the traps arranged for him, and bring his whole party safely into camp, having succeeded in capturing a dozen of prisoners and destroying several boats and a considerable amount of contraband property, during their absence.

The line of the river we were engaged in picketing during this time, embraced an extent of twenty-five miles, making the duty of the regiment, which numbered scarcely three hundred men for duty, very severe. But we lived in a "land flowing with milk and honey," and good cheer, in part, made up for hard work. This beautiful and fertile country, being plentifully supplied with poultry, milk and eggs, which were readily obtained in exchange for sugar, coffee and salt; and not unfrequently, as is the habit of soldiers, in sections not eminent for their loyalty, with exchange all on one side. And as the spring advanced the river swarmed with shad, herring and other choice fish, of which the Yankees soon invented means of catching more than they could use, so that when at length the order came for our exodus, we might have felt even loath to leave these fair meadows, had not the cannon's roar wafted to our ears from Marye's heights, the Wilderness and Chancellorsville, reminded us that the contest for another year had opened and we must prepare to bearour part.

At dark, on the evening of the 8th day of May, we commenced withdrawing our pickets and bidding adieu, alike to good living and the fair damsels of secessia who graced these regions with their charms, though regretting most to leave the former, as soldiers very readily learned to discriminate between the real and the visionary. We stored our haversacks with hard tack and salt junct, and about 11 P. M. were on the road to Falmouth.

Marching all night, at sunrise we found ourselves winding along over hill and hollow, through old camps and brush strewed clearings, toward Potomac creek bridge.

May the 18th, marched to U. S. Ford, and picketed along the river until the 28th, then moved to Warrenton Junction, and established camp. Here we were again engaged in picketing, but the duty was slight, and the regiment, during the eleven days of it uninterrupted stay here, was principally engaged in refitting, recruiting its horses, and preparing for active operations, which were soon to follow.

June the 8th, marched toward the river and encamped within a mile of Kelley's ford. June the 9th we crossed the river early in the morning and participated in the Battle of Brandy Station. See annexed official report of Colonel John P. Taylor.

"Head Quarters 1st Penna. Res. Cavalry, Warrenton Junction.
June 12, 1863.

"Lieut. Wm. P. Lloyd,

A. A. Adjt. Gen. 2nd Brig. 3d Div. C. C.

Lieutenant:—"I have the honor to respectfully submit, in brief review, the part my regiment took in the late cavalry fight at Brandy Station, Va., June 9, 1863.

On Monday, the 8th, the Cavalry Corps, commanded by General Pleasanton, according to orders, left this place at 2, P. M.; the first and fourth divisions commanded by General Buford, taking up a line of march leading to Beverly ford.

"The second and third divisions commanded by General Gregg, proceeded to Kelley's ford; both commands arrived at the different fords about dark, and bivouacked for the night.

"Before sunrise the following morning, the roar of cannon told us that the "ball had opened" at Beverly ford. General Gregg's command immediately proceeded to cross the river. Colonel Dufie, commanding the second division, taking the advance, followed by the third division, and thus proceeding to Stevensburg, about four miles from Kelley's ford. At this point, General Gregg, leaving Colonel Dufie with his command to protect his left flank and rear, proceeded with the third division on a road running parallel with the river, leading direct to Brandy Station. The Second Brigade, composed of the First Pennsylvania, First New Jersey, and First Maryland regiments, commanded by Colonel Wyndham, took the advance, followed by the First Brigade, commanded by Colonel Kilpatrick.

"No sooner had we arrived at Brandy Station, on the left and rear of the enemy, than their guns were opened upon us, at a range of one thousand yards. Our battery was immediately placed in position and engaged their guns, while Colonel Wyndham hastened to attack with his cavalry. One battalion of the First Maryland, led by Major Russel, charged upon their battery, followed by the remainder of the First Maryland, led by Lieutenant-Colonel Deemes, and the First New Jersey led by Colonel Wyndham in person. At the same time swinging my regiment around to the right,

"I led a desperate charge upon their left and rear, coming up to the Barbour House, in which was *General Stuart, staff* and *body guard,* surrounded by cavalry, with whom we spent thirty minutes in hand to hand conflict, killing and wounding and bringing away with us a number of prisoners, among whom was General Stuart's assistant adjutant-general, captured but a few feet from the renowned General Stuart himself. In this entire charge and conflict my men depended alone upon the cavalryman's true weapon, and tested the true merit and power of the sabre.

"At this stage of the fight, the enemy being heavily reinforced, we were compelled to give way, disputing every step to our new line of battle, where Colonel Dufie joined us with the Second Division. About this time Colonel Wyndham, having been wounded, was obliged to turn over his command to me, and my regiment to Lieutenant-Colonel Gardner.

"The enemy failing to attack us in our new position, the whole command moved off to the right, toward Rappahannock Station, where we again engaged the enemy with our artillery, and ordered the First Pennsylvania to support the battery, the enemy quickly replied, and a brisk artillery duel ensued, lasting nearly two hours, when I received orders from General Gregg to report immediately with my command to General Buford, at Beverly ford. With the First

Pennsylvania in advance, I pushed on rapidly and reported to General Buford, who immediately ordered me to his extreme right, where we, for the third time, engaged the enemy; and the First Pennsylvania displayed its usual bravery, in unsaddling a number of the enemy, and driving them back; thus having disputed possession of the river, and night coming on, we quietly crossed to the north side of the river and bivouacked for the night.

"I cannot close this brief review, without more especially speaking of the behavior of my officers and men, for all seemed to vie with each other in deeds of daring; and I could have desired no greater effort on the part of any one.

"I would beg leave to mention the gallant conduct of all my field officers,—Lieutenant-Colonel D. Gardner, Major Wm. T. McEwen, Lieutenant Charles C. Townsend, adjutant of my regiment; the latter having been on sick list for some time, and still ill, was at his post, during the entire engagement, rendering invaluable service.

"Major J. M. Gaston was not with the regiment, being at the time, on detached service, at Division headquarters."

ADDITIONAL SKETCH OF THE BATTLE OF BRANDY-STATION.

The 7th of June was spent in the hurry and bustle of preparation. Haversacks were stored, cartridge boxes filled, horses shod, the sick sent back, and all the usual preparation for active campaigning gone through with.

Then commenced the irksome and wearying delays incident to the moving of troops. Momentarily expecting the order to move, and yet hour after hour passing, and still not off. Evening came and night passed, and "reveille" awoke us to another day's expectancy. But we were relieved at noon. The bugle at division headquarters sounded the "general," tents were soon struck, saddles packed, and the regiments of each brigade massed in close column, when, after an hour or two's more delay, awaiting our trains to get on the road, "the advance" was sounded. Slowly pursuing our way through the heat and clouds of dust raised by the march of a division of cavalry over parched and arid fields, we at length reached the vicinity of the river, and at nine P. M. bivouacked for the night, about a mile from Kelley's ford.

The unusual precaution taken to prevent all unnecessary noise, betokened that we were in the neighborhood of the enemy, and might soon expect an encounter. In pursuance of previous orders, we were roused from our slumbers at three o'clock the next morning, and before we had finished our hasty breakfast, the thunder of Buford's cannon, borne on the calm morning air from Beverly ford, where he had already commenced crossing his division, brought us to the saddle, and soon we were drawn up on the river bank, around Kelley's ford, awaiting our turns to cross.

Meeting but little opposition from the enemy, in half an hour we had passed the river, and were pressing forward into the interior. Dufie's 3rd brigade having the advance, after proceeding some miles from the river, turned off in the direction of Stevensburg, while our (Wyndham's) command, moved rapidly forward, towards Brandy Station, with orders to find the enemy, and at once engage him. These were just the orders for our gallant and dashing brigade commander. Moving forward at a brisk trot, the First New Jersey Cavalry in front, the First Pennsylvania Cavalry next, and Martin's battery, and the First Maryland Cavalry bringing up the rear. In less than an hour we had reached the vicinity of the station, and our advance guard was engaged with the enemy's skirmishers.

Hurrying our columns from the wood through which the road had led for the last two miles, Colonel Wyndham formed his brigade in columns of regiment, in the open field east of the Station, and heading the First New Jersey in person, at once ordered the whole line to charge. Our sudden appearance on the flank and rear of the enemy took him somewhat by surprise, and for some minutes the hills and plains beyond the railroad, swarmed with galloping squadrons of "graybacks," hurrying to new positions, as their line of battle was being changed to meet our attack.

The First Maryland, with squadron A and B from our regiment, were ordered to move down on the Station, while Colonel Wyndham led the New Jersey against a battery on the heights beyond the railroad, and the balance of our regiment directed its operations against the Barbour house, a large Virginia Mansion, situated on a high knoll just beyond the railroad, and about half a mile north of the Station.

The field now presented a scene of grand and thrilling interest. A whole brigade of cavalry "in column of regiment" moving steadily forward to the attack on our side, while the enemy's cavalry, having completed its new formation, stood in glittering lines, awaiting the assault, and his artillery stationed on every hill, with rapid flash and continuous roar, belching forth its concentrated fire on the advancing columns.

But still, with undaunted firmness, the brigade, in sublime array, moved forward, first at a steady walk, then quickening their pace to a trot, and again as the awful space between the battle fronts, rapidly shortened, the gallop was taken, and as the crowning act of the grand but terrible drama, and when our line had closed on the enemy until scarce fifty paces intervened, the order to charge rang along our front; in an instant a thousand glittering sabres flashed in the sunlight; from a thousand brave and confident spirits arose a shout of defiance, which, as it rung from squadron to squadron, and was caught up by rank after rank, mingling formed one vast, strong, full-volumed battle-cry; and every trooper, at the same time rising in his stirrups, and leaning forward to meet the shock, dashed at headlong speed upon the foe. First came the dead heavy crash of the meeting columns, and next the clash of sabre, the rattle of pistol and carbine, mingling with the frenzied imprecation, the wild shriek that follows the death blow, the demand to surrender, and the appeal for mercy, forming the horrid din of battle. For a few brief moments the enemy stood and bravely fought, and hand to hand

and face to face raged the contest; but quailing at length before the resistless force of our attack, and shrinking from the savage gleam and murderous stroke of our swift-descending sabres, at length broke and fled in confusion.

Following him up, soon the whole plain for a mile in extent was covered with flying columns, engaged in a general melee, which continued, until the enemy, coming up with reinforcements, we withdrew and reformed.

When the First Pennsylvania Cavalry emerged from the woods, at the opening of the action, it was formed facing, and about half a mile from the railroad, and immediately on the left and supporting our battery. Scarcely half the regiment had gotten into position, when the enemy opened a battery, at point blank range, from the eminence of the Barbour house, hurling with great rapidity shot and shell into our ranks. When we moved forward it was to storm the position, and, if possible, capture the battery. As we marched straight forward toward the smoking cannons' mouths, they first saluted us with spherical case, and as the distance grew less, hurled grape and canister into our faces. But undaunted our line moved on, and would, doubtlessly, have taken the guns, had it not been broken in crossing an intervening ditch, which enabled the battery to move off before the regiment could be crossed. Once beyond the ditch, we formed ourselves at the foot or the base of the heights, forming under a heavy fire poured on us from the garden, yard and buildings surrounding the mansion, and half of the regiment, led by Colonel

Taylor, moved on the house from the front, while the other, with Lieutenant-Colonel Gardner at its head, swung around on its left and rear, and both wings dashing impetuously forward, soon cleared the enemy from the intervening space, and held possession of the ground.

An incident may be here noted illustrative of how utterly the Southern chivalry detest and dread the rough arguments of cold steel, when wielded by the Northern mechanic's sinewy arm.

Just as we were raising the hill, in our charge, a bold and audacious rebel rode forward from their ranks and called out, "Put up your sabres, put up your sabres, draw your pistols and fight like gentlemen;" but the mechanics, farmers and laborers of Pennsylvania placed too great confidence in their tried blades and the iron nerves of their right arms, to follow his advice, and soon these kid-gloved gentry blanched and shrank from the weight of their sturdy strokes.

We here met the flower of Stuart's cavalry, composed of his own body guard, and White's celebrated battalion and though unaware at the time, had stormed and carried his headquarters; this we learned from his adjutant-general who was among the prisoners taken.

June the 10th we returned to camp at Warrenton Junction, and resumed picket duty at that place.

On the afternoon of the 13th were again on the march. Halting near Warrenton, Companies A, B and C, Captains Wm. H. Patterson, R. J. McNitt and Lieutenant R. S. Lawsha, with Captain Wm.

Litzenberg in charge of the detachment, was sent forward to picket in the direction of Sulphur Springs and Waterloo, and remaining here until nine P. M. of the 15th, when the regiment quietly withdrew, and marching all night, reached Manassas Junction the next morning, where, in a few hour after, it was joined by the pickets.

BATTLES OF 20TH, 21ST AND 22D, FROM ALDIE'S TO ASHBY'S GAP.

The division having concentrated here, was supplied with rations, forage and ammunition, and after a day's rest, took up its line of march on the morning of the 15th, and moving westward, over the old Bull Run battle ground, struck the Centreville pike, and reached Aldie on the afternoon of the 17th. At dark on the 18th, we received orders to move down the east side of the mountains to Thoroughfare Gap, and hold it until relieved. Starting in a violent thunder storm, we groped our way through blinding darkness, over a miserable road, arriving at Hay Market at one A. M., stood "to horse" until morning, and then found the Gap. Relieved the following night, by the Second Corps, we rejoined the division on the morning of the 21st, at Aldie. Here Stuart's whole force was again met by our cavalry corps, and after two days' desperate fighting was forced back a distance of fourteen miles, and his routed and scattered columns pushed into the gaps of the Blue Ridge.

Our cavalry never displayed more determined and persistent courage than during these memorable actions. Stone fences, with which this country is covered, rocks, ravines, woods, ditches, buildings and every thing available for defence was held by the enemy, with a stubborn tenacity only excelled by the dashing bravery of our troops. As often as dislodged from one position he rallied on the next, holding it until again forced back by our resistless charges.

As our division acted as reserves, we were not engaged until the morning of the 22d, when we were ordered to the front, and covered our retiring columns from Upperville back to Aldie; the enemy following in force, pressed heavily on our brigade, the rear guard. The First Pennsylvania Reserve Cavalry held the left, and the First New Jersey the right of the pike, and although they were several times during the day attacked with great vigor and determination by the enemy, as often hurled back his charging columns in confusion.

At Brandy Station, Stuart's vaunting legions received their first lesson of the prowess of the Yankee cavalry, and here the finishing stroke, which reduced them to that point of inefficiency and worthlessness of which General Lee complained so bitterly in his official report of the invasion of Pennsylvania. The Cavalry Corps, taking position again on the heights around Aldie, the enemy made no attempt to push further

CAMPAIGN INTO PENNSYLVANIA.

Remaining at Aldie until the 26th to protect the crossing of the infanty and trains at Edward's Ferry, then moved forward toward the Potomac.

The regiment, as the extreme rear guard, was the

last to quit Aldie, and reached Leesburg about dark. Resuming march again next morning, we reached the river about ten, A. M., at Edward's Ferry, and crossing at two, P. M., drew up in close column of squadron on the Maryland shore.

This was the first time the regiment had been north of the Potomac since its first advance into Dixie, October the 10th, 1861. Its operations having been confined to an area of about seventy miles square, extending from Fredericksburg and the northern neck of Virginia on the east, to the Blue Ridge on the west, and from the Potomac on the north to the Rappahannock and Rapidann rivers and Shenandoah Valley on the south and southwest.

So often had this section of the sacred soil been traversed by the marching and couter-marching of the regiment, that every road, lane, and by-path were as familiar to us as the localities of our own homes. There was scarcely a town in the whole stretch of country around which we had not engaged the enemy, and more than once had the streets of some, as Warrenton, Aldie, Salem, and Culpepper, rung with the clatter of our charging squadrons, as we hurried the flying enemy from their vicinities; scarcely a place dignified with the name of village, which was not marked as a skirmish ground; a cross road at which we had not stood post, or a fordable point on the Rappahannock, from Port Conway, on the east, to where it dwindled to a mountain brook in Western Virginia, or on the Rapidann, from its mouth southward to Madison Court House, that we had .not guarded. So that when once freed from the barren wastes and the putrid air of this war-cursed region, it was not without emotions of joy that we again, after twenty months' absence, pressed a friendly soil, and once more breathed the atmosphere of loyalty, although we had come to roll back the tide of invasion from our own homes, and protect our own hearthstone from a ruthless foe.

At dark, on the same evening, we again commenced our march northward, passing through Poolesville and Barnesville, and reaching Urbana at daylight, halted to breakfast. Resuming march again, crossed the Monocacy river at the junction, and halted about eleven, A. M., a mile east of Frederick city. Here the regiment was detailed on special service at corps head-quarters, and ordered to the city to do provost duty. Leaving two companies, G and L, Captain F. P. Confer and Lieutenant H. S. Gaul, for provost duty, the regiment again moved forward on the afternoon of the 29th, reaching Middleburg at two, A. M., the 30th. Again on the road at daylight, arrived at Taneytown on the afternoon, and encamped in a strip of woods a short distance beyond.

BATTLE OF GETTYSBURG, PENNSYLVANIA.

At ten o'clock, P. M., July the 1st, resumed march northward, and traveling all night, reached the battlefield at nine, A. M., of the 2d, and took a position, as support for the reserve artillery of the cavalry corps, immediately in rear of the left centre, and remaining here all day, were withdrawn a mile to the rear at night.

Toward evening of this day, a fierce assault was made on the left wing of the battle line, which caused it to waver for a while before the fury of the onset; but the Fifth Corps coming up, just in time, a charge from the Pennsylvania Reserves, hurled the enemy back, retaking not only the ground lost, but pushed our line forward a half mile beyond the original position.

Returning to our former post, on the morning of the 3d. The battle opened at daylight on the right, and raged fiercely for several hours, but the centre and left remaining inactive until about two, P. M., when the enemy, in his last desperate effort, hurled forward the concentrated weight of his force on our centre and left. The action opened here again with redoubled fury, and with the view of opening a way for his advancing columns through our left centre, a point just in advance of the position occupied by the regiment, he poured a converging fire of more than one hundred guns on our line.

The regiment, though not engaged, was exposed to the full force of the terrific storm, but continued in its position until withdrawn from the range of that blasting withering stream of death. Moving a short distance to the rear, we remained until the enemy's massed columns were rolled back in confusion and defeat from the fiery front of our battle-line, for the last time, and the shouts of victory, first starting from Cemetery Hill, were caught up by division after division, and echoing from line to line and corps to corps, until the hills and woods and the whole broad country, covered by our vast army, rung with one long, loud shout of triumph; a shout that filled all hearts with rejoicing, that made the wounded forget their anguish, and which, as it fell on the ear of the dying, brightened once more the glazed eye with life's sparkle, and wreathed once again the pallid countenance with the smile of joy. And well might every heart rejoice. The day was won. Victory was ours. The rebel hordes were beaten back. Pennsylvania was rescued from the foul grasp of traitors, her fair domain spared the blighting curse of sweeping armies, and our nation's Capitol saved!

At sundown we received orders to withdraw from the field, and find grazing for our horses. Retiring some two miles to the rear, we turned into a field of grass, unsaddled and turned loose our jaded and almost famished horses, had supper, the first meal we had been permitted to prepare for two days, and wrapping our blankets about us, and lying down, though pelted by a dashing rain storm, were soon enjoying an uninterrupted and refreshing night's sleep.

Still raining next morning, and continued most of the day. Though our Nation's Birthday, all was quiet, every one appearing exhausted by the straining tension, to which both mind and body had been subject for the last three thrilling and momentous days, and the severe and wearing services of the two weeks previous. Enemy still in position beyond Gettysburg, but no movement of importance in front, all seeming, with common consent, to be spending the day in resting and resuscitating their wearied and exhausted powers.

Resuming the march again on the 5th, retraced our steps through Taneytown, turned southward through Greenesville, crossed the Doublepike and

Monocacy rivers, and halted for the night a few miles east of Emmetsburg, and near Creagerstown. As we passed through this section, the people assembled from all the neighboring districts "to see the army," and never did soldiers enjoy the luxuries of richly stored pantries than did the Union troops in passing through this fertile region. As we moved on, toward evening reports were brought to us that a heavy body of the enemy's cavalry was moving down the Emmetsburg pike. Halting before we reached the pike, we sent forward and soon found the rumor to be idle talk.

Next day, the 6th, we moved a mile or two forward, and within sight of Creagerstown, and as the regiment was alone, and in charge of eighteen pieces of artillery, the reserve of the cavalry corps, it was thought advisable not to move further without more support, halted and remained until next day, awaiting orders.

Marched back through Frederick city on the 7th, and halting for an hour to receive rations and forage, proceeded over the mountain to Middletown, and stopped just beyond for the night. Rained very heavily and found great difficulty in procuring camping ground for the regiment in the darkness.

On the afternoon of the 8th, moved forward to the base of South Mountain.

On the road again on the morning of the 9th, crossing South Mountain, on the old Sharpsburg road, and over the battle-ground of the year before. On the summit, a stone pillar erected, marks the spot where General Reno fell, and moving on to the outskirts of Boonsboro', bivouacked for the night. Remained here during the 10th, and on the 11th was relieved from duty with the reserve artillery, and ordered to report again to corps head-quarters. Moved up to the headquarters and encamped in a wood on the bank of the Antietam creek.

Rejoined the brigade again on the 12th at Boonsboro', where we encamped and remained two days, awaiting the concentrating of the divisions

While at Frederick city, Company A, Captain William H. Patterson, and Company B, Captain William Litzenberg, commanding the squadron, was temporarily detached as an escort for army headquarter's train, until July the 4th, when the squadron was ordered to report to Major-General Sedgwick, and formed the advance skirmish line of the Sixth Corps, in its pursuit of the enemy to the bank of the Potomac, at Williamsport, where it was relieved and rejoined the regiment at Boonsboro' on the 12th.

RETURN TO VIRGINIA.

The morning of the 14th again found us in the saddle, with our faces turned southward, and at eight, A. M., the Division took up its line of march toward Harper's Ferry, where, crossing the river over a bridge of pontoons, we formed close column, just beyond Bolivar, the upper town, and halted for the night.

In a slight skirmish, just after passing the river, our advance, a squadron of the First New Jersey captured a rebel colonel. Squadron I and K was sent forward about a mile from town, to picket the approaches to it.

At sunrise the next morning, the advance was again commenced, the Second Brigade in front. Proceeding some two miles forward, on the Winchester pike, the command turned to the right, and by the river road, reached Shepherdstown at noon, and immediately established a strong skirmish line encircling the town, as the enemy had shown himself in considerable force at different points. During the afternoon, the town was searched, and a considerable quantity of bacon, with other stores which had been collected for the rebel army, found and distributed to the command.

BATTLE OF SHEPHERDSTOWN, VIRGINIA.

Our column not resuming the advance, and the enemy apparently not disposed to make the attack, the night and the next morning up to eleven o'clock, passed without any hostile demonstration having been made on either side. But shortly after this, the enemy, doubtlessly having been reinforced, began to display a bolder front, and about noon the rattle of carbines on the right and rear of the town, where the Second Brigade was formed, gave evidence that the skirmishers were engaged. The artillery also soon opening, in less than half an hour the whole right had become engaged, though not a shot had been fired from our line, which extended from the left of the Second Brigade, eastward and nearly parallel with the river.

But we were not to remain idle long; the enemy's

first point of attack, as is generally the case, was but a feint, to conceal his real intention, and suddenly opening eight pieces of artillery on our left, he directed a succession of vigorous and heavy charges against it with the view of breaking the line, but our cool and gallant commander, General Gregg, had too often played the chess of battle to be caught in this manner. A sufficient force, well protected by a high stone fence and thick wood, was in position to meet the attack, and gallantly resisting every effort, at length drove him back.

Foiled in his object here, he again turned his attention to the Second Brigade. Renewing his attack on its lines with redoubled energy, and our regiment, which thus far had acted as reserve, was ordered to its support. Crossing an open space of nearly a mile, in face of the enemy's batteries, and turning down the Charlestown pike, and moving along it by column of fours, a half mile further in direct line with a battery, sweeping its entire length, we took up the position assigned us.

Companies I and K, Captains McGregor and Williams were immediately dismounted and sent to the right, and Company C, Captain McNitt, Lieutenant H. McClenahan and Lieutenant Nelson; and Company D, Captain McDonald, Lieutenant Holbrook and Lieutenant Walker to the left to reinforce the skirmish line, while the balance of the regiment present, consisting of Company A, Lieutenant Kelly, and Lieutenant Wilson; Company B, Captain Litzenberg and Lieutenant Buzby; Company E, Captain Newman and Lieutenant Akers, and Company F,

Captain Davidson and Lieutenant Lucas remained mounted with sabres drawn to charge, in case the enemy should break the advance line. The regiment remained in this position for two hours and a half, and until the action ceased at dark, although all the while subject to heavy fire of infantry at close range, and a cross-fire of artillery. As night approached, the enemy became more desperate in his efforts to force our line, and made charge after charge on different points of it with both cavalry and infantry, aided by storms of grape and canister, but the rapid and deadly volleys of our carbines as often forced him back. At midnight we were withdrawn, and the Division marching through a drenching rain storm, reached Harper's Ferry at nine A. M. next day, and encamping on the sloping declivities of Bolivar Heights, remained until the 19th.

AGAIN EAST OF THE BLUE RIDGE.

At the sound of the "general," shelter tents were struck, saddles hurriedly packed, and two P. M. found us mounted in line and ready again for the advance.

Crossing the Shenandoah and passing around the base of Loudon Heights, we moved forward some six mile, and forming close column of squadron, picketed our horses and bivouacked for the night.

On the road again at an early hour, next morning, moved slowly forward as rear guard, and in charge of the train, reaching Perryville, on the Leesburg and Winchester pike, at dark. Here Companies G and L joined the regiment, from Frederick city.

At noon on the 21st, arrived at Hillsboro', encamped

in a wood, and remained until the 23d, having our horses shod, and the regiment supplied with rations, forage and ammunition.

Dress parade in the evening of 22d.

A short respite of two days, and again southward bound, reaching Snicker's Gap, the Brigade halted, and our regiment was sent forward to picket Ashby's Gap, relieving the Seventh Michigan Cavalry, a squadron was sent forward to the gap, and the balance of the regiment encamped in a wood, in rear of the village.

On the night of the 24th, the pickets reported the enemy approaching, and the regiment was turned out, but it proved to be a small party of guerrillas prowling around the lines. On the 25th, a small party under charge of Captain R. J. McNitt, made a scout along the mountain, north of the gap, and succeeded in securing several horses, which had been brought by the enemy from Pennsylvania, and placed there in concealment

Withdrew the pickets at dark on the 26th, Sunday evening, and taking up the line of march, passed through Upperville, along the Aldie and Middleburg pike, to Middleburg, where we joined the brigade at two o'clock next morning. At five, A. M., again in column of route, moving over roads rendered almost impassable by the recent rains, through Salem and Thoroughfare Gap to New Baltimore, and thence along the pike to Warrenton, encamping at nine, P. M., about two miles east of town. Weather exceedingly warm.

Marched at seven o'clock next morning, the 28th,

to Warrenton Junction. Returned to Warrenton next day, and went into camp. Had anticipated a few days rest here, but were again on the road on the morning of the 30th, and with the division crossed the Rappahannock a short distance above Waterloo, and moving south some eight miles, to Amisville, establishing camp, commenced picketing toward Jefferson and the Hazel river.

On the 31st, Captain J. Newman, with portions of E and F companies made a reconnoisance to Hazel river, and found the enemy in force on the other side. At three o'clock on the morning of August the 1st, our line of pickets was ordered to be advanced to the Hazel river; meeting no opposition, they reached it in an hour, and when day dawned and the enemy discovered our line stretching across the country so near them, betook themselves to very rapid preparations for an attack, but after remaining in battle line for some time, and finding that we made no further advance, went into camp again, and some of them coming down to the river, which was scarcely ten paces wide, made stipulation for neither party to fire, as long as no atcempt was made by either to cross the river.

Scouted on the 4th, in the direction of Culpepper, and found the enemy in force, a short distance beyond the river. Again in the saddle for a scout at three, A. M., on the 5th, and crossing Hazel river at daylight, we advanced to Muddy run, some six miles beyond.

The enemy, who had permitted us to advance thus far without offering any opposition, now commenced throwing heavy columns around on our flanks, with the view of cutting us off. But discovering his object, we deployed a heavy rear and flank guard, and commenced a rapid return; and though greatly outnumbered by the enemy, who made frequent efforts to reach our rear, but were beaten back and foiled in every attempt, we finally reached the river, after an hour's sharp skirmishing, without the loss of a man.

Returned to the north side of the Rappahannock on the 8th and encamped near Sulphur Springs; the whole regiment sent on picket.

On the 9th, Lieutenant George W. Lyon, of Company I, with a party of sixteen men, crossed the river on a scout, and being cut off by the enemy, was supposed captured; but making his way safely through the enemy's lines, joined General Buford's command and returned to the regiment next day by the way of Beverly ford.

Continuing on picket until the 15th, when we moved to Warrenton and established camp. Here Company H, Captain W. S. Craft, Lieutenants T. C. Lebo and E. C. Forsyth, which were detailed on special duty at headquarters, Sixth Army Corps, on the 22d of last February, rejoined the regiment. During its absence, the company was present with the Sixth Corps at the battle and storming of Marye's heights, in rear of Fredericksburg, May 3d, and on the 2d and 3d of July, at the battle of Gettysburg.

A scout on the 18th to Salem by Campanies A, B, and I, under command of Captain McGregor, and on the 19th by the whole regiment to Greenwich and

Gainesville. Re-crossed the Rappahannock on the 24th, and moved to Jefferson on picket, and returned to Warrenton on the 27th.

The 1st, 2d, and 3d of September were spent on regimental and brigade drill. The regiment sent on picket again on the 4th; established a line from Rappahannock, northwest along Carter's creek, where an outpost was surprised on the night of the 6th, and Lieutenant George W. Lyon and Corporal Barre were killed, and four men captured. On the morning of the 10th the brigade started from camp at Warrenton on a scout, in the direction of Bull Run Mountains. At Salem our regiment was detached and sent by way of White Plains to Middleburg. A party of thirty men, with picked horses, under charge of Captain R. J. McNitt, were detailed as an advance guard. Scouring the country in every direction in search of Moseby and his guerrillas, until noon the next day, when we returned to camp without any captures.

BATTLE OF CULPEPPER.

Breaking camp on the morning of the 12th, we moved to Jeffersonville. "To horse," sounding at daylight on the morning of the 13th, in half an hour the division had again taken up its line of march. Our brigade, crossing Hazel river at Oak Shade, moved forward to Rixlieville; and halted to await the arrival of the second brigade, which had turned off at a ford about a mile to the left.

Coming up at nine, A. M., it took the advance and

moved off in the direction of Culpepper, we following immediately after.

Meeting the enemy at Muddy run, a sharp skirmish ensued, which lasted about a half hour, when the enemy fell back and the division crossed. Resuming the advance, the second brigade now became engaged in heavy skirmishing, which lasted all the way to Culpepper, which we reached about noon. Here our brigade was ordered to the front, and the regiment being the advance guard was immediately deployed as skirmishers. Company K, Lieutenants Kennedy and Morgan, being on the extreme right, and next in order; Company D, Captain McDonald, Lieutenants Holbrook and Walker, Company G, Captain Confer and Lieutenant Reed; Company E, Lieutenant Akers; Company F, Lieutenants Lucas and Greenlee, formed the right wing, and on the right of the Culpepper and Cedar Mountain road. Company A, Captain Patterson and Lieutenants Kelly and Wilson; Company B, Captain Litzenberg and Lieutenant Lawsha; Company C, Captain McNitt and Lieutenant Nelson, forming the centre and immediately adjoining the road, and on the left in regular succession. Company I, Captain McGregor; Company L, Lieutenants Gaul and Buxton; and Company M, Lieutenants Sample and Wright. Company H not being armed with carbines, remained as a support in rear of the centre, ready to charge when occasion might require it. Formed in this manner, the advance was at once commenced, the regiment moving forward on horseback. But scarcely had we ascended the first range of hills when the enemy opened a scathing fire on us from woods and thickets, which told fearfully on both men and horses, exposed as they were, and was rapidly thinning the lines, when the horses were ordered to be sent to the rear and the men to fight on foot. Dismounting on the spot and forming again under the galling fire the enemy were all the while pouring upon them, and the order to charge being given, the whole line, stretching over the hills for half a mile, moved forward as one man, rushing over the open field, without a stump or stone for shelter, on to the enemy, who from his cover poured his fire into their faces at point blank range. And thus they fought for three successive hours, step by step, for four miles, only quitting the field when relieved, their ammunition being exhausted. Not a man, from the time the regiment went into action until it was relieved, was seen, along the whole length of the line to waver or swerve from his post; the line officers on the skirmish line with their men, encouraging them with their presence in the numerous and successive charges, and Colonel Taylor and Lieutenant-Colonel Gardner, the only field officers present, with Chaplain Beale, acting adjutant, mounted, were targets for a hundred rifles, riding from point to point along the line wherever their presence were required.

The regiment never did its duty better, or showed itself more worthy of the place it holds on the roll of honor of its State, than on this occasion. Every copse of woods, stone fence, thicket and ravine along the route fought over, was taken advantage of by the enemy, and held with a stubbornness and bravery worthy of a better cause.

But as often as he rallied and made a stand, the First Pennsylvania Reserve Cavalry charged his defences, carrying them by storm, and forcing him back to new positions.

Following this action, the regiment was engaged in skirmishing every day until the enemy was driven beyond the Rapidann, on the 17th; and then, after a respite of twelve hours, was again on the skirmish line along the river, where it remained for twenty-four consecutive hours, all the time exposed to a harassing fire from the enemy's sharpshooters in rifle-pits on the opposite bank.

Returned to Culpepper on the 18th. Again at the Rapidann on the 22d, on picket duty. Relieved on the evening of the 24th, and reached Culpepper on the 25th.

On the morning of the 26th again on the march northward, crossing the Rappahannock about noon, we reached Catletts at night, and went into camp. Continuing here, guarding the railroad and scouting the country for some miles west of it until October, when we again moved to the Rapahannock and picketed its north bank in the vicinity of United States ford. Crossing at Kelly's ford on the 11th, and encamped at Rappahannock Station. Re-crossed the river and moved to Fayetteville on the morning of the 13th, and in the evening to Auburn.

BATTLE OF AUBURN.

Here our pickets were attacked early in the morning of the 14th by the enemy in force. Heavy fighting commenced immediately, and although the enemy pushed with great vigor to break our lines, and reach the wagon trains in our rear; we held him at bay until they passed out of danger. Our regiment being in the extreme rear at this place, we only escaped being entirely surrounded and cut to pieces by a heavy infantry force, which opened fire on both of our flanks simultaneously, and commenced rapidly closing in on all sides of us, by the heroic bravery and cool, determined action of the regiment.

When it emerged from the fiery circle, the converging columns of the enemy were scarcely a hundred yards from its flanks, at the point of egress; and although raked from the rear by grape and canister, and saluted on both sides by volleys of musketry, the regiment marched quietly out in "column of fours," as calmly as if passing in review, not a horse moving faster than a walk, nor a man leaving his place, and except those struck down by the hail of death which swept over them from all sides, not a gap was seen in the ranks. A sublime spectacle it was, indeed, and as soon as the regiment had cleared itself from the encompassing dangers, Captain H. C. Weir, A. A. G. of the division, the whole of which had witnessed the thrilling scene, rode forward from the side of General Gregg, and proposed three cheers for the First Pennsylvania Reserve Cavalry. They were given on the spot, and with a will too, that showed no spark of jealousy, but how keenly a soldier appreciated his comrades' bravery, and with an energy that rung as shouts of defiance in the ears of the baffled foe.

After the action of the morning, the regiment continued skirmishing, as our army slowly fell back, and was again hotly engaged in the evening at Bristow Station.

Thursday, the 15th, continued skirmishing all day, and until we reached Bull Run. On the 16th, still engaged in skirmishing, crossed and re-crossed Bull Run five times during the day.

At Wolf Run shoals, the regiment being relieved for a few hours, the horses were unsaddled, and the men betaking themselves to cooking, washing and the various other little occupations which demand a soldier's attention during the occasional short respites from duty, and brief halts on the march of such vigorous campaigns as this, and soon became dispersed in the neighborhood of the camp. But they were not permitted to enjoy this pleasure long. A party of rebel cavalry, which had been lurking in our rear and remained concealed in the woods, awaiting this moment when we were least prepared for an attack, came sweeping around a point of woods a few hundred yards from camp; but the alarm being immediately given, the bugle sounded "to arms," and in a moment all in camp had snatched up their arms, and were ready to receive the audacious intruders, who not fancying the greeting a hundred carbines were waiting to give them, wheeled their horses before coming in range, and made off again without accomplishing any thing further than giving some of the men a sharp chase to camp, and causing the regiment to "saddle up," without giving it an opportunity to pay them for their trouble. Picketing along Bull Run, and scouting the country beyond, until the 21st, when the regiment moved to Gainesville, and the next day through Warrenton, to the vicinity of Sulphur Springs, where we established camp. Engaged in picketing here until the 6th of November, on the evening of which we marched for Rappahannock Station, and reaching Bealton next morning, halted until afternoon, then moved toward the river and encamped. Moved to Fayetteville on the 9th and established picket line in direction of Warrenton and Sulphur Springs, and remained until the advance over the Rapidann.

On the night of the 17th, Moseby, with one hundred guerrillas, charged the picket reserve of the first battalion, commanded by Captain Davidson, killing one man, wounding one, and capturing three with some horses; but was so roughly handled, that he soon made off with several of his number wounded. The attack was made by about fifty, in charge of Lieutenant Turner, dashing on Captain Davidson's head-quarters, and F Company, from the rear; while Moseby, with as many more, engaged the pickets in front. But the reserve, though dashed on without a moment's previous notice, while lying around their fires, were not to be overcome so easily as the enemy doubtlessly supposed. Seizing their carbines and pistols, and rallying in rear of their camp, immediately opened a fire, which joined by one or two volleys from Captain McNitt's squadron, Companies A and C, which encamped near by, was soon on the ground, sent the modern "Knight-errantry" scampering over the hills in undiscriminate confusion.

On the afternoon of the 21st, Moseby again paying us a visit, waylaid some teams near Fayetteville, and carried off a number of mules. Our regiment being

7*

ordered in pursuit, struck his trail about a mile east of Warrenton, and pushed forward at a gallop, to overtake him if possible, before reaching the mountains. Following him in this manner, scarcely half an hour in his rear, to Thoroughfare Gap, the night came on, and no longer able to trace his course, we were compelled to abandon the pursuit. We, however, captured one of his party and several horses which lagged behind, and in a house near the gap found the equipments, arms and overcoats of three others who had left so hastily as not to be able to take them along; arrived at camp at two, A. M.; having ridden a distance of thirty miles through a drenching storm of rain.

ADVANCE OVER THE RAPIDANN RIVER.

On the morning of the 23d, our line of pickets was withdrawn, camp broken up, and by four, P. M., we were on the road with the brigade, moving toward Rappahannock Station, reaching Bealton at ten at night, we bivouacked a short distance beyond the railroad. Marching the next morning we joined the Second Brigade at Morrisville, where we halted to be supplied with rations and forage. Next morning, the 24th, our brigade following the second, the whole division moved toward the Rappahannock, which we crossed about noon, at Ellis' Ford, and halted some four miles beyond, picketing toward the Rapidann. Here, a rain storm setting in, we remained the next day and the day following, delayed, as we supposed, by the inclement weather.

Resumed the march on the 26th, the Second Brigade still leading the advanee, we pushed forward toward the Rapidann Meeting but little opposition, crossed the river at Ely's Ford, and moved forward toward the Frederickburg and Germania pike; halted until night, then continuing the march eastward in the direction of Spottsylvania Court House, crossed the Fredericksburg and Culpepper and the Fredericksburg and Orange Court House plank roads, advanced some ten miles further, and halted at eleven P. M.

BATTLE OF NEW HOPE CHURCH.

In the saddle again at daylight, the First Brigade leading the advance, we struck the Fredericksburg and Orange Court House plank road again at Parker's store, a point about fourteen miles from the latter place. Here we were joined by the Pennsylvania Reserves, the advance of the Fifth Corps, and the whole column moved forward toward Orange Court House. Some four miles on, the enemy's advance was met, which our skirmishers pushed slowly back to New Hope Church, about two miles, when they were next met by his main body, consisting of infantry, cavalry and artillery, the advance of Ewell's Corps. Our regiment being ordered to the front immediately after the commencement of the action, moved forward with the view of charging on horseback, but after remaining in position a short time, awaiting to meet a dash, threatened by the enemy on our skirmishers, dismounted, as the dense woods which covered the country prevented any efficient operations on horseback, and prepared to fight on foot

As soon as the order to advance was given, the

whole line, with a shout, dashed forward, broke the enemy's lines and sweeping around on the flank, captured twenty-eight of his infantry with muskets and bayonets in hand, while our only arm was the carbine and pistol.

We then established a line and held it against every effort of the enemy to break it, for two hours, and until relieved by the Pennsylvania Reserve Infantry.

This was the second time, at Fredericksburg and here, that the regiment was relieved when the press of battle became too heavy for its light lines, by this famed group of regiments, whose brilliant achievements have carved for them a name so high on the scroll of honor,—the family of the Pennsylvania Reserves, in which we claim a sister part.

Additionnl Particulars.—Our line was formed, the right consisting of Companies K, Lieutenant Kennedy, and Company L, Lieutenant Buxton, resting on the plank road; the centre, Company G, and part of H Company, Captain Confer and Lieutenant Reed, and the left, E, Captain Newman and Lieutenants Akers and Herrick; D, Lieutenants Holbrook and Walker, and M, Lieutenant Wright, extending to the railroad. Squadron B and I, Captains Litzenberg and McGregor and Lieutenant Lawsha remaining mounted, were employed as skirmishers on the extreme right, and the portion of Company H not supplied with carbines, left in charge of led horses.

After the regiment had been dismounted and thus formed, the order to deploy as skirmishers was given, and although on the open ground and under heavy fire, the movement, "left into single rank" was executed as calmly and correctly as on the parade ground. Then in steady, regular line, the advance commenced toward the wood by which the rebel line was covered, but scarcely had ten paces been made, when the enemy, rising from their concealment, with a hideous discord of sickly, screeching yells, so peculiar to them, poured a volley into our line. Without a recoil, or even a halt at this sudden and unexpected attack, the regiment no sooner caught sight of the enemy than some one in the line shouted, "charge," and with one full determined cheer, forward it dashed over ditches, stumps and brush, and through the enemy's first line, completely breaking his formation, capturing the men or compelling them to fling away their arms in the attempts to escape, and forcing the whole line back, fully three hundred yards, and until checked by his reserve infantry.

At the same time that the First Pennsylvania Reserve Cavalry started forward on the eharge, the First New Jersey Cavalry, (that first of Cavalry regiments,) joining lines, immediately on its right, and fighting side by side, as on many a field before, catching up the shout that rung from our ranks, at once joined in the advance, and on swept the twin regiments, each vieing with the other in deeds of daring, and yet each generously awarding to the other the meed of praise.

At dark the regiment was ordered back to Parker's store, and passed a rainy night in a low, marshy wood, and the next day moved some three miles west to the Wilderness tavern, on the Fredericksburg and and Culpepper pike to picket. On the afternoon of the 29th, the camps of the Third Pennsylvania and

First Massachusetts Cavalry were attacked by Hampton's Division, and a portion of the Third Pennsylvania forced back to our line. We immediately formed line along the plank road, and awaited the enemy's coming, but he drew off without any further demonstration. On the 30th we again marched back to Parker's store, where another dash of the enemy brought us again into battle line, but it proved to be only a scouting party, and we were soon withdrawn and went to making ourselves comfortable around large fires, as the weather was extremely cold.

The evening of the 1st of December again found us at the Wilderness tavern, where we stood to horse all night, awaiting the army, which was now falling back to pass.

The last of the infantry having gone by, our regiment being the rear guard, we commenced at nine, A. M., of the 2d, slowly withdrawing, hurrying up the stragglers before us, and skirmishing with the enemy, who was hovering on our rear. In this manner we reached the river at noon, crossed and rested in the woods on the west side.

Picketing along the Rapidann until the 6th, and moved to Brandy Station. Remained here until the 10th, and then marched for Warrenton. Arrived on the 12th and went into winter quarters, encamping just east of the town, in a beautiful and healthful situation, and by the 20th had excellent winter quarters completed.

On the 22d the regiment, under command of Captain Davidson, Colonel Taylor being at the time in command of the division, and Lieutenant-Colonel Gardner in command of the brigade, marched with the Sixth Ohio Cavalry to Amisville, to join a portion of the second brigade in a scout to Luray valley; but not reaching that place until some hours after the second brigade had passed by, the detachment, in pursuance of instructions, returned to camp.

On the night of the 25th, Captain Newman, with one hundred men, in conjunction with a similar detachment from the First New Jersey, made a scout to Salem; the party capturing two guerrillas.

January the 1st, 1864, the regiment marched with the division in a reconnoissance to the Shenandoah valley, but on arriving at Front Royal, on the evening of the 2d, found the Shenandoah river too high from recent rains to ford, and were unable to proceed further. Bivouacking on the bank of the river for the night, next morning commenced return to camp, reaching it on the afternoon of the 4th. During the four days out, the weather was very severe, and the command suffered much from cold and exposure.

Scout on the 8th to Salem.

February the 17th, a detachment of one hundred men, Captain McGregor, Lieutenant Kennedy and Lieutenant Kelly, from the regiment, with an equal number from the First New Jersey, and smaller detachments from the First Massachusetts and Third Pennsylvania Cavalry, started under command of Lieutenant-Colonel Kester, (First New Jersey Cavaly,) on a scout to Ashby's Gap, in the vicinity of which they surprised and captured twenty-eight of Moseby's guerrillas, with a number of horses, arms, and equipments, and destroyed a considerable quantity of stores.

The following is an account of the affair, furnished by Captain T. C. McGregor:

"At midnight of the 17th we started from the rear of Warrenton, where the detachment had assembled. The night was exceedingly cold, yet by daylight we were thirty miles on our way, and had already begun to bag our prisoners. About ten, A. M., of the 18th inst., Moseby's whole crew rallied and made a desperate attack, evidently for the purpose of recapturing the prisoners A part of the First Pennsylvania Reserve Cavalry turned upon them, and never did they get so complete a whipping in so short a time as on that frosty morning, near Ashby's Gap. Had it not been that our horses were jaded while their's were fresh, we would have added largely to our number of prisoners. After destroying their head-quarters, hospital stores, a large quantity of whiskey and commissary stores, and capturing a quantity of clothing and a mail, we started on our return, bringing off twenty-eight prisoners and over sixty horses. Once more they attempted the rescue of their comrades at Upperville, but the First New Jersey Cavalry taught them another severe lesson. In this affair, Captain Hart, of the First New Jersey, was slightly wounded, and this was the only casualty on our side. We reached camp the same night, after having marched about sixty-five miles in less than twenty-four hours. Such is cavalry service in winter."

Marched February the 27th, seven officers and two

hundred men from the regiment, under command of Captain Davidson, with other detachments from the division, joined General Custar in a raid to Charlotteville, on the left and rear of Lee's army. Were absent five days and marched a distance of one hundred and seventy-eight miles.

March the 7th, scout of fifty men, under command of Captain McGregor, sent to New Baltimore.

The 8th, another scout of fifty men to Sulphur Springs and Waterloo, under charge of Lieutenant Holbrook.

At eleven, P. M., the 9th, one hundred men, Captain Litzenberg, Lieutenants Forsyth and Buxton, with one hundred men from the First New Jersey, made a scout to Salem.

19th. Captain McNitt and Lieutenant Lucas, with one hundred men, made a scout to Salem, charged a party of the enemy, driving them from the town, and capturing one of their number.

21st. Captain Confer, with seventy men, made a scout to Sulphur Springs; another next day, by Captain Litzenberg, Lieutenants Herrick and Buxton, with one hundred men.

To sum up, in brief, the duties of the regiment have, during the present winter thus far, been the most constant, exhausting service it has ever performed. An extensive and exposed line to guard by vigilant picketing, constant annoyance from bands of guerrillas, with numerous and fatiguing scouts, have kept the men almost constantly on duty.

Of scarcely four hundred men present for duty with the regiment, it has furnished a daily aggregate of ninety-five men for picket duty, with nearly an equal number for scouts, guards, and other details. This severe service, with the exposure incident to a cavalryman's duties in winter, has told heavily in reducing the effective strength of the regiment. But spring is here again. Another winter's storms have been met and borne on the tented field, and the vernal winds with the strengthening beams of an April sun are rapidly preparing the roads for travel. For weeks the work of preparation has been hurrying on to reach its present consummation. Worn out and condemned horses, arms and accoutrements have been supplied by new ones; daily inspections and reviews have detected and sought to correct or rememedy every evil and deficiency in the ranks; all visitors to the army have been sent home, none but soldiers are wanted here now; the haversack is packed, the cartridge-box refilled, the sabre, the musket and the cannon cleansed and burnished, and we stand ready for the field.

Day by day we await the notes of bugle from Division Head-quarters, sounding the "general," and at the same time announcing the opening of the spring campaign of the Army of the Potomac for 1864.

The ranks that were thinned by disease and battle during the last year, have been more than filled by recruits. Another directing spirit has been assigned the control of our giant war machine, the laurelled Chieftain of the West, and the army will go forth as buoyant with hope, as determined in resolve, and stronger in numbers, more efficient in discipline, and schooled by experience and hardship—in nerve and sinew more potent in its operations, and more reliable in its endurance than ever before.

Here we pause in this imperfect summary of the operations of the regiment for thirty-two months of its life. Four more months still remain, and it will have fulfilled the period of its organization. What events remain to be chronicled in this brief, but doubtlessly active period, before its history closes, or the old organization merges into a new one, stamped with the honored name of Veterans, are yet hidden in the future.

THE CAVALRY, ITS ARMS, ETC.

During the first fifteen months of the war, much of the cavalry being scattered through the army, attached to divisions and corps, and employed as escorts, guard and advance pickets, &c., and little of it being so organized as to be prepared to act independently, (though its duties were as severe as they have ever been since,) its opertions were so diffused as to afford it little opportunity of showing what might be done if its services were properly applied. And as a natural consequence, it began to be looked upon as an almost useless appendage to the army. But the collecting and organizing of the cavalry of this army, at least, during the winter and spring of 1863, into brigades, divisions, and a separate corps, with horse artillery attached, have enabled it, by the services of the past year, to earn for itself an honorable position beside the other arms of the service, and to establish a rank in efficiency and in importance second to none in the army. Though the peculiarities of the country in which we operate have compelled the change of our light armed troops to dragoons or heavy cavalry; yet, wherever they have been privileged to meet the enemy as cavalry proper, in the charge and with the sabre, they have shown themselves superior to him in every respect, as Brandy Station, Aldie, Gettysburg, and various other fields will attest. The experience, however, of the last campaigns have clearly established the supremacy of the carbine as the cavalryman's most effective weapon—compelled, as he is, in this country of forests, thickets, fences, ditches and stone walls, to fight, much of the time, on foot—the pistol being seldom used, and generally only in close contest, when the sabre or carbine are lost or fail; and it is scarcely decided whether its effectiveness overbalances its cost to the Government and the inconvenience of carrying it.

CAMPAIGNING OF 1864 AGAINST RICHMOND.

Services of the regiment during the last five months of its term, viz.: April, May, June, July and August, 1864.

The month of April, up to the 21st, was chiefly spent in drilling, reviews, &c. Early this morning, however, the long expected order to break camp was received, and soon all were engaged in the hurry and bustle of preparation. By eleven, A. M., our winter habitations had disappeared, and in an hour more the division was on its way toward Warrenton Junction. Halting three miles from the Junction, we found fine camping-ground, and the division was soon disposed along Turkey Run, a small stream which afforded facilities for watering.

Here we remained until the 24th, when the regiment was detailed for picket duty, and marched at 5 A. M. for Morrisville, eighteen miles southeast, and near the Rappahannock river. Establishing a picket headquarters at this place, and connecting with the Tenth New York Cavalry at Grove Church, four miles further down the river, and picketing the various roads leading to the river, and also back into the country, we remained until the advance across the Rapidann. While engaged in this duty, the command was greatly annoyed by guerrillas and dismounted cavalrymen, who crossed the river for the purpose of procuring horses, and concealing themselves in the woods and thickets, watched their opportunity to fall on and capture pickets and small scouting parties. On the night of the 28th, Major R. J. Falls, with seventy-five men, made a scout to Falmouth, twenty-five miles distant; and on the 2d of May, Captain Davidson, with one hundred men, paid that place another visit; but neither party found any force of the enemy this side of the river, and consequently met with no incident worthy of note.

May 3d, withdrew our pickets at eight A. M. Crossed the Rappahannock at Kelly's Ford, and rejoined the division at Richardsville, near the Rapidann. In the saddle again at one o'clock next morning, moved slowly forward toward the Rapidann, which we reached at four, and crossing at Ely's Ford, halted until after daylight. Contrary to expectation we met but a small force of the enemy here, merely a picket-guard, which was scattered by a few shots, and our crossing left unopposed. Resuming our march at sunrise, we halted for an hour or two at Chancellorsville, and then pushed forward some six miles, and encamped for the night near Pine Creek Church. The Second Brigade, which led the advance from Chancellorsville had some slight skirmishing toward evening.

FIGHT AT TODD'S TAVERN.

Next morning, the 5th, moved slowly forward toward Spottsylvania Court House, forming repeatedly and feeling for the enemy. At two P. M., we received orders to move rapidly forward and take possession of Todd's tavern, some three miles in advance of our present position. Arriving at that point we found a brigade of our infantry in battle line, and the Third Cavalry Division, commanded by General Wilson, moving back in haste and confusion, hotly pushed by the enemy. Our brigade was immediately thrown forward to cover the rear of the Third Division, and meeting the enemy in a charge, at once became sharply engaged, but soon succeeded in checking his lines, and hurrying him back faster than he had advanced. Following him up with charge after charge, and though obstinately contesting the ground he was at length compelled to fall back across the Po river, some three miles distant.

In this engagement, Colonel Taylor, with seven companies, acted in conjunction with the brigade, while Lieutenant-Colonel Gardner, who, just previous to the opening of the action had been sent with the other five companies down the Spottsylvania Court House road, with instructions to push forward to that place. This, however, he soon found himself unable to do, as he was met by a heavy force of the enemy, when scarcely two miles out, and his own party with a battalion of the First Massachusetts Cavalry sent to his support heavily pressed for some two hours, and until relieved by the Second Brigade.

At dark the regiment was placed on the skirmish line, where it remained until four, P. M., next day, being engaged in occasional skirmishing during the whole time.

Retired some three miles on the evening of the 6th, and at noon of the 7th again moved forward to our former position at Todd's tavern.

SECOND FIGHT AT TODD'S TAVERN.

The First Division being in order of battle, immediately commenced the attack, and our brigade moving forward, took position on its left. Shortly after arriving on the ground, the regiment was ordered out to meet an advance the enemy were making on our extreme left. Dismounting two battalions, and joining the Sixth Ohio, which connected with the left of the First Division, we pushed forward on the Spottsylvania Court House road. A charge was immediately commenced along our whole line of battle, and the enemy, although stubbornly resisting the movement for a time, was at length compelled to give way, retiring in such haste as to leave all his dead and wounded on the field, and a number of prisoners in our hands. Encamped on the battle-field at night.

Next day, the 8th, recrossed Pine creek, and at night moved back to the Fredericksburg plank road, where the Cavalry Corps was concentrating. The regiment on picket in the direction of Chancellorsville.

THE RICHMOND RAID

May the 9th, marched with the Cavalry Corps on a grand raid, in the direction of Richmond. Crossed, during the day's march, the Massaponax, Ny, Po and Ta rivers.

FIGHT AT CHILDSBURG.

When about ten miles out, the First Division, which led the advance, met a party of the enemy, who continued harassing our advance and right flank during the entire day, growing more bold and persistent as evening came on. About five, P. M., the rear, which was guarded by our brigade, became heavily pressed, and a charge on the Sixth Ohio, which constituted the extreme rear guard, forced them back on our regiment, which formed its support. Some little confusion was at first occasioned by the sudden attack, but our line was soon formed, and a sharp fight commenced, which lasted until dark, when we withdrew our skirmishers and continued the march. Halted at midnight on the north bank of the North Anna; and brought into the saddle again at three o'clock in the morning, by a shower of the enemy's shells. Crossing the North Anna at daylight, marched to Beaverdam Station, which the First Division had destroyed, and crossing South Anna river at Ground Squirrel

Bridge, about four, P. M., encamped a few miles beyond.

Heavy skirmishing in front and on the right flank during the day. Wednesday, 11th, fighting, but moving steadily forward. Our brigade detached and sent to Ashland, some eight miles distant, destroyed the station, and after a severe skirmish, in which the First Massachusetts Cavalry lost heavily, rejoined the division at one P. M. The First Division and Second Brigade of our Division were heavily engaged at Hungary Station and Yellow Tavern during the entire afternoon, but handsomely repulsed the enemy at every point. General Custer's Brigade capturing two pieces of artillery and a number of prisoners. Our brigade, being held in reserve, was not engaged.

BATTLE OF MEADOW BRIDGE, OR RICHMOND HEIGHTS.

Marching all night, passing down the Brock road to within two and a half miles of Richmond, and daylight of the 12th found us, with the First Division, crossing the Chickahominy river, at Meadow Bridge, the Third Division following next in order, and our division drawn up between Richmond and the river to guard the crossing. The First Division became hotly engaged as soon as it reached the north side of the Chickahominy, and the Second, our Division, was assailed on three sides as soon as it was sufficiently light to make the attack. Every effort was made by the enemy to break the lines of our division and push us back into the river and swamp. But as often as he came up, he was driven back with heavy loss. The fighting continued thus, the enemy charging, time after time, only to be hurled back, until about eleven A. M , when, apparently completely disheartened by his repeated repulses, he withdrew, and we quietly crossed over the bridge, reaching the north side of the Chickahominy about three P. M. Continuing the march, the corps passed through Mechanicsville, and encamped beyond Gaines' Mills. Friday 13th, marched ten miles and encamped at Bottoms Bridge. Crossed Bottoms Bridge on the 14th, and reached James river at Haxall's Landing. Our regiment, having the advance of the corps, was sent forward to open communication with the gunboats. Mistaking us for rebel pickets, they opened on us, and gave us several shells before we could make ourselves known, but fortunately the shells did us no harm. Remained here during the 15th, 16th and 17th, but moved out at seven P. M. of the 17th, and marched all night. Crossed Jones' Bridge on the 18th and encamped at Baltimore Cross roads. Left Baltimore Cross roads at five A. M., the 20th, and marched to Cold Harbor. Marched to the White House on the 22d. Crossed the Pamunky river on the 23d, on the railroad bridge, and marched *via* Brandywine to Ayletts. On the 24th marched to White Chimneys, and on the 25th rejoined the army at Chesterfield Station, and encamped three miles to the rear, having been absent about seventeen days. Moved again at two P. M. of the 26th; marching all night, and crossing the Pamunky on pontoons, at Hanovertown, at daylight of the 27th.

BATTLE OF HAWS' SHOP, OR ENON CHURCH.

Marched at eight, A. M., of the 28th, to Haws' shop. The regiment being ordered out on a scout, met the enemy in less than half a mile from the brigade, and at once engaged him. Having attacked a squadron of the Tenth New York Cavalry, which was on picket, he was hurrying it down the road, when his charge was met by the head of our column. The first battalion Companies A, C. G and H, commanded by Major R. J. Falls, moving off the road; the third battalion, Companies B, K, D and M, commanded by Captain Litzenberg, charged, clearing it and hurrying the enemy back half a mile, to his support. Our line was then formed, the third battalion holding the road, the second battalion on the right and the first on the left of it, and the whole regiment immediately dismounting under a heavy fire, advanced to the attack. The division now also coming up, the action soon became general, and the fighting at once assumed the most desperate character.

At point blank range the contending parties fought for seven hours, neither able to carry the other's position, but each determined to hold its own. So rapid and constant was the firing, that during this time the regiment, though scarcely two hundred of it being engaged, expended upward of eighteen thousand rounds of ammunition. Many of our carbines, also, became so heated as to render them for a time entirely useless; and so the fighting continued until half past four, P. M., when the division, being reinforced by General Custar's brigade of the first division, our whole line dashed forward in one of the most gallant charges of the war, carrying every thing before it, driving the enemy for three miles and strewing the track of his routed columns with hundreds of his dead and wounded. Too much cannot be said in commendation of the steadiness and gallantry of the regiment in this, one of the fiercest and most obstinate actions in which the cavalry has been engaged. Occupying the centre of the line, and holding the road where the heaviest of the fighting occurred, our loss was, consequently, very severe.

Withdrew from the field at midnight and encamped near the river.

At four, P. M., of the 29th, marched to near New Castle and encamped.

At two, P. M., 30th, marched to the front. The regiment set out at dark to picket at Bethesda Church, on the flank of the army. Relieved at two, P. M., of the 31st; in camp two hours and then ordered to the front again, standing to horse all night.

Wednesday, June the 1st, the brigade moved to the support of the first division at Cold Harbor, and by heavy skirmishing, held the enemy until relieved by the infantry, when we moved some four miles to the left and rear, and encamped.

FIGHT AT BARKER'S MILLS.

On the 2d moved around on the left flank of the army and engaged the enemy's infantry at Barker's Mills. The regiment was ordered from the rear of the column to the front and extreme right to charge a battery, but after making the attack the battery was found to be protected by a swamp in front, and supported by a heavy force of infantry, sheltered by earthworks. The regiment, however, moved forward under a raking fire of artillery and infantry, and took up a position in close range of the enemy's works, and held it until our heavy lines of infantry came up. We here lost heavily in both men and horses. Marched in the evening to Bottom Bridge and encamped. Remained in camp during the 3d, and received supplies. Shelled the enemy on the opposite side of the Chickahominy this evening, and on the 4th our camp was shelled by the enemy in return; one man wounded and several horses killed in the regiment. Our camp shelled again on the 6th, but no damage done.

THE TREVILLIAN RAID.

Marched at seven, P. M., toward the Pamunky river, crossed on pontoons, near New Castle, at midnight. Received supplies on the 7th, and continued marching at nine, A. M., and encamped near Ayletts. Marched at five, A. M., of the 8th, and encamped near Pole Cat Station.

On the 9th, crossed the railroad at Pole Cat Station, passed through Childsburg and New Market, south of Spottsylvania Court House, and encamped at N. E. Creek.

On the 10th, continued our march toward Gordonsville, and encamped on the North Ann river. Crossed the North Ann on the 11th, the first division and part of the second heavily engaged along the railroad from Louisa Court House to Trevillian Station, and succeeded in forcing the enemy back seven miles, and capturing four hundred and eighty prisoners. The regiment being the extreme rear guard, was engaged in picketing and protecting the trains.

Relieved from picket on the 12th, and joined the brigade at Trevillian Station. Was ordered to the front at three, P. M., to report to General Torbert, commanding the first division, and placed in support of a battery, was exposed to heavy shelling, but not otherwise engaged. At dark ordered to the extreme right under a heavy fire of artillery, but not being needed, was returned and sent back to our brigade. The corps, after accomplishing the destruction of the railroad for several miles, commenced withdrawing at nine, P. M , and marched all night. Crossed the North Anna at nine, A. M., 13th, and encamped between Plentiful river and Horseforemost river. Resumed the march at five, A. M., of the 14th, and encamped at Catharpen river, on the Fredericksburg road. On the 15th marched by Spottsylvania Court House to within three miles of Guinea Station. On the 16th crossed the Ta and Mattapony rivers, passed through Bowling Green and encamped twelve miles beyond, near Mattacocy creek. Marched through Newtown and Clarkesville on the 17th, and encamped on Roy's creek. On the 18th passed through Walkertown and King and Queen Court House, crossing Anseaman, Tide, and Court House creeks, and encamped near Corbin's Mill, on the river road leading to West Point. On the 19th, countermarched *via* King and Queen Court House, Walkertown and Clarkesville, and encamped at Dunkirk, on the Mattapony. Crossed the Mattapony on pontoons, on the 20th, and marched *via* Ayletts and King William Court House to White House Landing. The regiment being the advance of the corps, encamped on the river bank near the railroad bridge.

ENGAGEMENT AT WHITE HOUSE.

The enemy having appeared in force on the opposite side of the river, commenced an attack early this morning on the defences of the place, shelling the corps train which was parked here awaiting our return, and compelling its removal to the north bank of the river, so that when we arrived here, instead of the short respite we had anticipated after the long and exhausting services of this memorable raid, we found the enemy again in our front, whose force must be met, forced back and held at bay until our trains could be moved to the south side of the James river, where the army had gone a week before. Accordingly, at two, A. M., of the 21st, we were aroused from our half finished slumbers, and hastily equipping ourselves for a fight on foot, left our horses in charge of a guard, and crossed the river with the division to repel an attack expected at daylight; but after awaiting several hours, it was found that the enemy had withdrawn and taken up a position on the elevated ground some two miles back from the landing. Our brigade at once returned to camp on the other side; mounted and re-crossing the river, moved forward to the support of the second brigade, which had advanced on foot to feel the enemy's position.

The first division having crossed the river during the morning, formed on the left of the second, continuing a line which encircled the landing a mile or two from the fortifications. Though the enemy were seen to manœuvre large bodies of troops in our immediate front, no attack was made, and every thing remained quiet, except some slight skirmishing along the line of the second brigade, until four, P. M. The regiment, which, with the brigade, had been lying in reserve up to this time, was now dismounted and marched a mile across the country to make an attack on the flank of the enemy, and capture or compel the removal of a gun which was annoying our skirmishers. Arriving at the point designated, our line was formed and supported by a single mounted squadron of the First New Jersey Cavalry, the advance commenced along a narrow strip of cleared land, skirted on all sides hy dense woods, Pursuant to orders, but contrary to the judgment of the officers of the regiment, it was pushed rapidly forward without the protection of skirmishers on either flank, until it had reached the wood at the farther end, fully half a mile distant. The result was, that scarcely had the attack commenced in front, when the enemy advanced from the woods on both flanks and opened a galling fire on our rear. To retrace our steps, and precipitately too, was the only course left. The whole regiment was fairly entrapped, and though three officers and thirty-five men were left killed, wounded or prisoners in the hands of the enemy, it only saved itself from total destruction by that steady coolness which has won it honors on so many fields. Fighting furiously as it withdrew, the enemy's flanking columns were kept back until clear of his encircling fire, when a new line was formed and his advance permanently checked. This brief but unfortunate affair, one of those inexplicable occurrences incident to the chances of war, and for which no one is responsible, being the first that has fallen to the lot of the regiment, a fact which reflects the highest credit upon the efficiency and military abilities of its officers, caused much regret, especially as so many of our brave comrades were sacrificed without any material advantage having been gained, Instead, however, of any censure being attached to either the officers or men, as the former led the latter only where they were ordered to go, the action of the regiment was highly complimented by General Gregg, division commander, and it was congratulated by the entire brigade on its comparatively fortunate escape. The earnest and candid manner, too, in which the men exculpated Colonel Taylor, Lieutenant-Colonel Gardner, and all the officers of the regiment from any blame in the matter, with the unswerving confidence the regiment has always awarded to the efficiency and ability of its officers, and which was here increased rather than diminished, was only equalled by the proud satisfaction with which the officers, in return, expressed their admiration of the gallantry and coolness of the men. At dark the regiment was withdrawn from the battle-field, and Captain Davidson, with his battalion, placed on picket, while the balance of the regiment bivouacked a short distance to the rear.

Marched at noon of the 22d, to Baltimore Cross roads, and took up a position, holding the roads for the protection of the wagon train, on its passage to the James river. Crossed the Chickahominy at Jones' Bridge, an the 23d, and encamped at Charles City. The regiment on picket at Hopewell Church.

BATTLE OF ST. MARY'S CHURCH.

The First Division, with the trains, passed on in our rear, toward the James river during the night and morning, while our division, this morning (the 24th) continued it advance on a road at right angles with the Charles City Court House road, and running parallel with the Chickahominy river, and some four miles from it. The Second Brigade, being in front, met the enemy's pickets about three miles out, and pushing them back a short distance, came on his main body in strong position, near St. Mary's Church. The Second Brigade at once formed its lines in an open field, the right extending across the road, and the left forming a semi-circle, until joined by the First Brigade, part of which was formed so as to extend the line parallel with the road a half a mile to the rear, and thus protect that flank, while the balance of the brigade, formed in column of regiment, composed the reserve.

The day, until half-past four, passed with slight skirmishing by the Second Brigade, and occasionally a sharp encounter for a few moments, when the enemy would throw a force forward to feel our lines, which he did at various points during the day. Suddenly, at this hour, however, apparently fully advised of our position and strength, he advanced, making a vigorous and simultaneous attack on our whole line. To meet this, the portion of our brigade in reserve was at once sent forward, and in less than twenty minutes after the attack had been made, the whole division was hotly engaged. It soon became evident that the enemy far out-numbered us; but the division, with its accustomed steadiness, fought him for fully two hours, and until overwhelming numbers, pouring in upon it from three sides, compelled its lines to give way and move hurriedly back.

But although assailed, as we afterwards learned, by the whole Rebel Cavalry Corps, supported by fifteen hundred dismounted men, yet such was the persistent courage displayed by the command, and the skill with which our retreat was managed, that in falling back six miles, the enemy failed to capture a single cannon, caisson, wagon or ambulance, and made prisoners of but few of our men. When the last general onset was made by the enemy, the regiment, which had been in support of our battery during the day, was immediately dismounted and sent to take a position on a commanding eminence, which enabled it, at the same time, to protect the battery and support the left of our line. The enemy having discovered the importance of the position, was hurrying forward at the same time to occupy it, but our boys, by hard running, reached it a few moments in advance, and by a volley or two pushed his columns back again to the shelter of the woods, where a constant and well-directed fire kept him, until our forces had passed by on the right, and all withdrawn from the field. The enemy coming down with a mounted force on our right and rear, just as the regiment commenced moving back, cut it off from the line of our retreating column; but by making a detour through the woods on our left, we soon succeeded in joining its rear, with which we continued until the enemy discontinued the pursuit, when we withdrew to Charles City Court House, reaching that place at eleven P. M. In this action, as in the three preceding ones, our loss was heavy as will appear by the appended list of casualties.

The regiment stood to horse during the night of the 24th, and shortly after daylight, moved with the division a short distance forward, and formed on the right of the First Division, which held the road leading to the battle-field of the day before. Ascertaining, however, that the enemy had withdrawn, the division marched at eleven A. M., toward the river, and established camp near Wyandott's Landing.

Here closed General Sheridan's second grand raid, the corps having been absent from the army nineteen days, and engaged in either marching or fighting the entire period, without a single day's respite. Crossed the James river on transports on the night of the 27th, and encamped three miles south of the river. Marched again at sundown of the 29th, and arrived at daylight at Prince George Court House. Resting an hour or two, moved forward to Blackwater creek and encamped. The regiment sent forward to picket the Petersburg and Jerusalem Plank road. July the 1st, rejoined the brigade at Templeton. Returned on the 2d, *via* Prince George Court House, and encamped near the City Point and Petersburg roads. Marched on the 4th, toward the James river and established camp near Light House Point.

Here we enjoyed the first pause of more than two days' length from the unremitting labors of the march and the battle-field since we crossed the Rapidann, on the 4th of May. Of the sixty-one days which had elapsed since the commencement of Grant's grand campaign against Richmond, fifty-four had been spent by the cavalry in either marching, scouting, picketing, or fighting. Being much of the time also in the immediate presence of the enemy, we were subject to that unceasing vigilance which exerts every energy to its utmost tension, and wears away the spirits and the strength more rapidly than the heavy toils of steady and constant labor; such as the slow, cautious and wearisome march, now halting, now marching again, now forming, dismounting and standing to horse, then remounting, changing position and forming again; aroused at night and hurried into line, to spend the drowsy hours until morning, in the saddle, hungry and jaded, a whole day without an opportunity of "cooking coffee," and then, when a moment's leisure is had and the tempting and grateful beverage is almost prepared, hurried away from the untasted meal to hours more of the fatiguing duty,—so that grateful indeed were these days of respite after two months thus spent.

ENGAGEMENT AT REAM'S STATION.

Broke camp again on the evening of the 11th of July, and marching all night, arrived at Prince

George Court House, at daylight. After an hour's halt to breakfast; continued the march, crossing the Petersburg and Suffolk Railroad and moving along the Jerusalem plank road toward Warwick swamp. When two miles from the swamp, the division halted, and our brigade taking a right hand road, moved off in the direction of Ream's Station. The regiment having the advance of the brigade, was ordered to deploy skirmishers and push rapidly forward to the station, some three miles distant. Our line was accordingly formed, Companies E and F deployed as skirmishers, and I and D, forming the advance guard. Advancing a few hundred yards through the woods, we met the enemy's pickets, when a brisk skirmish commenced, the enemy falling gradually back, first to his main reserve, and then to his battle line, which was established in a strong and commanding position beyond a deep and almost impassable ravine. Forcing our way across the ravine and gaining the high ground beyond, two battalions were immediately dismounted and engaged the enemy. The First New Jersey Cavalry, and one piece of artillery, coming up soon after, our line was advanced, and the enemy forced back to his second line of defence; but it not being the object on our part to bring on a general engagement, no more of the brigade was brought forward; and after several hours' hard skirmishing, by which the strength and position of the enemy were fully ascertained, we were withdrawn. Rejoining the brigade again at five, P. M , at the point we had left in the morning, we were ordered to the support of the Second Brigade, which had become engaged on the plank road, near Warwick swamp, but on reporting, our services not being required, we returned to the brigade and encamped for the night. Next morning, the 13tb, removed three miles to the left of the plank road and encamped. On the 14th the regiment was sent back to the plank road to picket, and during the night following was considerably annnoyed by the enemy, the outposts being several times attacked and driven in. Relieved at noon of the 15th we returned to camp, and on the 16th marched with the division back to Light House Point, and established camp near our former ground.

(Notes furnished by Assistant-Surgeon L. E. Atkinson.)

BATTLES OF MALVERN HILL AND LEE'S MILLS.

"After remaining in camp here ten days, engaged in light picket duty, the cavalry corps, on the afternoon of July 26th, received marching orders, and the First Pennsylvania left its camp at five, P. M., two hundred and twenty men strong, under command of Lieutenant-Colonel D. Gardner, Colonel Taylor having received a sick leave for twenty days. The sick were left in camp together with all dismounted men. By dark the regiment was fairly started on the march, and with the exception of a halt on the banks of the Appomattox at midnight, marched constantly all night. The Appomattox was crossed on a pontoon bridge, near Point of Rocks, and the column was headed toward the James, reaching that river about four miles above Bermuda Hundred at three, A. M.

"The Second Corps had preceded the cavalry, and

was now crossing the river on a pontoon bridge. By seven, A. M., it had all crossed, and the advance was already engaged with the enemy. The cavalry immediately followed, and after crossing, formed on the right of the Second Corps, with artillery in position, and every thing indicating that a battle was anticipated and prepared for. About noon General Grant rode along the lines. The entire day was spent in position, the enemy apparently indisposed to make an attack, and our lines not advancing. In the evening orders came to make ourselves comfortable for the night. At three, A. M., on the 28th, camp was aroused and breakfast cooked, and at daylight we advanced on the Richmond side of Malvern Hill. Our brigade had the advance of the corps. About nine,, A. M., we encountered the enemy's infanty advancing, and a battle at once ensued. The First Pennsylvania was quickly dismounted and advanced in battle line across a wide field to a forest on the other side. They had no sooner gained the forest than they were furiously attacked by a division of rebel infantry, and after a sharp action of about thirty minutes, and being entirely unsupported, were reluctantly compelled to retire. In this action three officers were wounded, three men killed, and fifteen men wounded.

"The rebels, after at first gaining an advantage, quickly retired, leaving their dead and severely wounded on the field; of the latter there was a very large number, more than equaling our entire loss.

"The cavalry having been relieved by the Second Corps, retired to the river, and our brigade having remained until night, re-crossed the river and left the horses on the south side. At nine, A. M., on the 29th, the regiment again crossed to the north side of the James, and threw up rifle pits in front of the brigade, our line now being a prolongation of the line of the Second Corps, we occupying nearly the same position held by us on the 27th.

"We remained in this until about twelve, P. M., when we returned to the south side of the James, and mounting, immediately took up the line of march for our old position in front of Petersburg. We reached the Appomattox about daybreak, and the men here, had time to cook breakfast.

"The river was then re-crossed on a pontoon bridge at Point of Rocks, as before, and the head of the column took the direction of the Petersburg and Weldon Railroad, and by two, P. M., had gone several miles to the left of the main army, in front of Petersburg. At this time the advance of our brigade had encountered the enemy's cavalry, strongly posted at Lee's Mills. After a sharp fight the enemy was dislodged, and precipitately retreated. The First Pennsylvania was in support of the battery and sustained no loss. Captain Williams' battalion was placed on picket in the front, in the evening, and remained until one, A. M., when it was relieved by a portion of the first division, and the regiment marched back about four miles toward James river and encamped.

"Between the period of leaving Light House Point and of going into camp at this place, the regiment marched five consecutive nights, and was engaged in the most arduous duty during the whole time. Continued picketing here until the 9th, when we returned to camp at Light House Point. Again on picket on the 11th."

(Notes furnished by Chaplain J. H. Beale.)

AGAIN NORTH OF THE JAMES AND BACK TO REAM'S STATION.

"Saturday morning at six o'clock, the regiment, after a night in the saddle, came in from picket to camp, at Prince George Court House, with orders to be "ready to move at four o'clock, P. M." The day was spent in busy preparation for the morn. Many were the speculations as to the destiny of the expedition, as "each breeze that swept from the north brought to our ears the clash of resounding arms." Many entertained the agreeable idea that we were about to be shipped to Washington. However, at five, P. M., the column moved off on the road leading toward the *river*. Colonel Taylor being absent on sick leave, and Lieutenant-colonel Gardner being unwell, the regiment was commanded by Captain Newman, and took its position for the day second in 'order of march.' As the column left the main road and wended its way across the "*Appomattox*," we well understood what was before us. A week's hard service of picketing, scouting, and the engagement of Gravel Hill, July 28, 1864, told us plainly what was before us. Consoling ourselves with the idea that what had been endured once could be borne again, we travelled on, and four A. M., on Sunday morning, found us on the north side of the *James river* about three miles below Deep

Bottom, where the Tenth Corps was already engaging the enemy, after a night's march as disagreeable as any in the history of the regiment, occasioned by *intense heat* and *dust,* which in the absence of any breeze, settled in almost impenetrable density along the entire line of march."

"Sunday, August 14th, eight, A. M., General Gregg's division of cavalry took position on the right wing of the Second Corps. The First Pennsylvania Reserve Cavalry took the advance of the division on the road leading to '*Gravel Hill,*' twin-sister to 'Malvern Hill,' overlooking an extensive and fertile plain between it and 'the James.' Our advance guard drove in the enemy's vedettes half a mile before we reached *the Hill.* Rushing on rapidly, the advance battalion, companies (A, C, G and H) commanded by Captain Confer, charged the height, where the enemy were strongly intrenched. But the charge was so rapid and determined that the enemy were completely routed, thus we gained their first line of works before a regiment of infantry, which they had in reserve, could come to their assistance. We continued to drive them half a mile further, when other regiments of the brigade came up, and, taking the advance, continued to drive them still further, when night put an end to fighting. In this engagement we had five (5) men wounded. At night the Second Brigade came up, and relieved the First Brigade, which lay in reserve during the night."

"Monday morning, the Second Brigade advanced and pressed the enemy back through a *dense wood,* while the First Pennsylvania supported the battery.

(There being but one battery to the division.)* Tuesday morning, the First Brigade moved out about two miles, on the Charles City Court House road, and took position on the right of the Second Brigade. Here the regiment remained on the out-post dismounted behind a strong line of works the enemy had thrown up when Grant made his passage across the James, until near night, when the Second Brigade was forced back, and we were compelled to contract our line, whereupon the Second Brigade had a severe fight; and the First Brigade relieved them at sunset, and re-established the same line held during the morning. The regiment remained saddled during the night. At two A. M., Wednesday morning, all hands must 'stand to horse,' in anticipation of a morning attack. Wednesday was spent in the same position, every man on duty until six P. M. The enemy by a flank movement compelled us again to abandon our position. But not until the regiment barely escaped being cut off, saved only by the length of the regiment in 'column of route.' The encircling flank of the enemy switching the rear of our regiment as it passed. Another night and the regiment again 'stands to horse' all night, and so remained until two P. M., we unsaddled for the first time since Tuesday morning. But we had scarcely obeyed orders to 'go into camp' when another order came, 'Be ready to move at five P. M.' Just as night was settling upon us a foaming rain doing the same, we recrossed the James with orders to report to army headquarters. Another all night of it. Thus passed the week of hard duty, in which we added to our roll of honor '*Gravel Hill*, No. 2. August 14. 1864."

SKIRMISHING NEAR REAM'S STATION.

At daylight on the 20th, the division left army headquarters, and moved forward to the Gurley House, drew up in battle-line, and remained in that position until dark, when a portion of the command was placed on picket, and the balance permitted to go into camp. Sunday 21st, the command in the saddle at early dawn, and advancing toward the Weldon Railroad. Reaching the road, the enemy were found in force a short distance beyond it, and heavy skirmishing immediately commenced and kept up during the entire day. The 22d and 23d were spent by the brigade in picketing beyond the railroad, with occasionally a slight skirmish. At dark, however, of the 23d, our brigade was relieved by infantry, and sent to the support of the second brigade, which was stationed along the Dinwiddie Court House road, and was then being heavily pressed by the enemy. Reinforced by our brigade, the division, after a sharp fight of an hour, succeeded in driving the enemy and retaining possession of the road. The 24th and 25th, until four P. M., passed without any hostile demonstrations by the enemy. But at this time he made another general assault, a last desperate effort to retake the road. Assailed in front and at the same time heavily attacked on the flank our infantry was at first compelled to retire, and suffered considerable loss, but, rallying, prevented the enemy from gaining any permanent advantage. The cavalry being stationed on the flanks was also hotly engaged. The First Brigade occupied a position on the right of the Second Corps and between it and the Fifth Corps, and the Second Brigade on the left of the Second Corps. The cavalry fought dismounted, as the marshy nature of the ground prevented the use of horses, and nobly sustained its enviable reputation. The regiment, although stationed on one of the most exposed portions of the line, fortunately escaped with but slight loss.

Withdrew on the 26th, some two miles to the rear, and were engaged in changing position from place to place along the railroad until the 29th when we established camp on the Jerusalem Plank road, near the left of the army.

On the 30th, the long and anxiously looked for order to report in the State of Pennsylvania to be mustered out was received. The 31st was spent in mustering for pay, and organizing the veterans and recruits, four hundred and one in number, into companies. They were formed into four companies, D, officered by Captain H. A. McDonald, Lieutenants H. Platt and J. W. Nelson; F by Captain J. H. Williams and Lieutenants Holbrook and Forsyth; L by Captain T. C. McGregor and Lieutenants Lebo and McDonald, and M by Captain H. S. Thomas, Lieutenants Morgan and Herrick. The whole composing the First Pennsylvania Veteran Cavalry Battalion and commanded by Major R. J. Falls.

Thursday, September 1st, the old members of the regiment, whose times had expired, took a farewell leave of the battalion remaining, and quitting the front, marched to City Point. After a necessary delay of two days employed in turning over quartermaster's and ordnance stores, the regiment was embarked on the steamer Claymount, and shipped *via* Fortress Monroe, Chesapeake and Delaware Canal to Philadelphia, where we landed on Monday the 5th, and were mustered out and discharged on Friday the 9th..

SYNOPSIS OF OPERATIONS IN THE CAMPAIGN OF 1864.

The brilliant operations of the cavalry in the campaign of 1864, against Richmond, will form a page in the chronicles of this great rebellion, not unworthy of a place side by side with the gallant achievements of the infantry and artillery, and the pen of the historian will record alike, in the same glowing characters, the heroic deeds of each arm of the service, as well as of the divisions, batteries and squadrons whose honor it is to share the fame of the grand old Army of the Potomac.

The efficiency given to the cavalry by collecting, organizing and forming it into a separate and independent body during the winter and spring of 1863, was fully attested by its operations in the campaign of the following summer and fall.

At Kelly's Ford, in March of 1863, the enemy first learned the concentrated prowess of the Yankee sabre, and again in June following at Brandy Station and Aldie, and in July at Hanover Junction, Gettysburg, and Shepherdstown. The reverses he met with in every instance where his cavalry was pitted in battle against our gallant squadrons, taught him that his boasted legions of chivalrous cavaliers could no longer cope with the dashing valor of the Yankee horse; and from this time until winter closed the operations of the year, he risked no more engagements singly and alone; but, as at Culpepper, Rapidann, Auburn, and New Hope Church, only fought when heavily supported by infantry. So that when the work of the year was finished and we returned to winter quarters, it was with the satisfaction that so far as the cavalry arm of the enemy's power was concerned in sustaining the rebellion, it was completely broken and demoralized.

During the winter, however, reports reached us that every effort was being made to recruit and strengthen his shattered battalions, and with such success too, as to promise a force of cavalry at the commencement of hostilities in the spring, equal if not superior to our own.

But the victories which have crowned the arms of Sheridan's Cavalry Corps in every instance where numbers placed the contending parties on even an approximate equality, during the four months of brilliant and continuous service since the crossing of the Rapidann, have again fully demonstrated our superiority, and even at this period of the season, when the year's operations are scarcely half finished have so broken his battalions and demoralized his troopers, that he dares not now meet us unaided by his infantry.

The unfavorable circumstances under which the operations of the regiment since the commencement of the present campaign have been sketched, being almost constantly on the march, have compelled the greatest brevity to be exercised, yet its services have been, if possible, more arduous, and its fighting, as the list of casualties will show, more desperate than during any previous period of its history.

The Cavalry Corps, headed by that gallant and dashing leader, Major-General P. H. Seridan, crossed the Rapidann as the advance-guard of the army, pushed forward through the Wilderness, and traced the lines along which our massed corps of infantry deployed their columns and fought that series of terrible battles which first taught vaunting rebeldom that the fastnesses of the Rapidann could be flanked, that the Army of Northern Virginia could be defeated on its own ground, and its commander outgeneraled by his own tactics. Meeting and defeating in two general engagements at Todd's Tavern, the enemy's whole cavalry force, our corps then took up its march around the flank and rear of the rebel army and moved straight forward toward his capital. Fighting the enemy in front, on both flanks and in rear at the same time, yet moving steadily on, its columns penetrated the outer defences of Richmond, and for half a day our cannon thundered their hoarse notes in the ears of her citizens, then coolly marching around her northern border encamped on the James river.

Two days rest, and then returning to the army, headed the grand flank movement which brought our army from the front of Lee's frowning entrenchments at Hanover Court House to his flank and rear at Cold Harbor; and by the successes of Haws' Shop, Cold Harbor, and Barker's Mills, traced again for the army its battle-lines until they reached the Chickahominy.

Quitting the army again as soon as our services were not further needed, our columns were headed for the heart of Virginia; and at Trevillian, after a week's exhausting marches, we again met the enemy in two days' battle. Accomplishing our object here, and then returning by a winding and circuitous route, met the enemy at White House and St. Mary's Church on the 21st and 24th of the same month.

Crossing the James river, and after a fortnight of hard service, fought a severe engagement at Ream's Station, then back across the James, were heavily engaged again at Malvern Hill on the 28th, and returning on the 31st, closed the month with a fight at Lee's Mill, on the extreme left of the army.

Ten days of August were also spent north of the James with the Second Corps, and then back again to the Weldon Railroad, ended the month and the term of service of the regiment, with a series of severe skirmishes in that vicinity.

FAREWELL ORDER.

Headquarters, First Pennsylvania Reserve Cavalry,
NEAR WELDON RAILROAD, August 31st, 1864.

(*General Order*, *No.* 18.)

OFFICERS AND SOLDIERS OF THE FIRST PENNSYLVANIA RESERVE CAVALRY:—You have now experienced three years of terrible, devastating war; you are familiar with its toils, its hardships and its scenes of bloodshed. During this time there has been no toil that your manly efforts have not overcome; no hardships that you have not courted for your country's sake; no field of strife too terrible to prevent you flaunting your banner in the face of your traitorous foes, and in every instance have you borne it off in triumph. Many have been the fields upon which you have distinguished yourselves by your personal valor. From your first victorious blood spilt at Drainesville down to that more green in your memory, such as Todd's Tavern, Childsburg, Haws' Shop, Barker's Mill, White House, St. Mary's Church, and last, but not least, upon the bloody summit of Malvern Hill, are still sounding in your ears and eternally engraven upon your hearts.

But you have now reached the goal of your worthy ambition; you have won for yourselves, your regiment, and your State, an invidious reputation.

Officers and soldiers of the First Pennsylvania Reserve Cavalry, allow me, on this the eve of our separation, to express to you my heartfelt thanks for your implicit confidence and ready compliance with every order and unflinching bravery upon every field I have had the honor to lead you. Your military career has been a brave and clear record, in which you have acquitted yourselves like men.

But the war is not ended yet. There are more battles yet to be fought, and more lives to be offered up on the altar of liberty. For this end some of you remain and many more of you will soon be back to battle in this your just and holy cause. But whenever you may answer to the "bugle's call," and upon whatever field you may strike the black shield of rebeldom, let the memory of your fallen comrades strengthen your arms and encourage your hearts, ever mindful that you were once members of the

First Pennsylvania Reserve Cavalry. May the God of battles and of mercy be your shield and protection.

By order of

J. P. TAYLOR,

Colonel Commanding Regiment.

W. P. LLOYD,

Adjutant First Penna. Reserve Cavalry.

ADDRESS OF COLONEL J. P. TAYLOR.

After the above order was read to the regiment, which had been formed by Lieutenant-colonel Gardner, Colonel Taylor made the following remarks:—

MY BRAVE COMRADES:—We stand to-day upon the threshold of an event, which, when we left our homes three years ago, the most prophetic heart scarcely dared anticipate the scenes then rife in our midst. Such as the memory of an insulted flag upon Fort Sumter, which cast a gloom of shame over every true American heart, and the blood of brothers spilt in the streets of Baltimore, as it were, sprinkled over every loyal heart in the North. The rushing of men to arms, and our souls inspired by the spirit of our fathers, nerved us to action, and from homes of comfort, luxury and ease we rallied in defence of our country.

Another turn of the kaleidescope found us marshalled beneath the proud ensign of our glorious Republic. No longer separate and distinct in thought and action, but the firm resolve of the farmer, the willing hand of the laborer and mechanic, the shrewd energy of the merchant, the potent influence of the student, all suddenly converted into the trained and disciplined soldier, with hearts that beat as one. What you were then, and what you have since proven yourselves, you owe to the mighty impulses of your first great and noble commander Colonel George D. Bayard; imbued with the influence of his mighty genius, you saw the star of his glory rising and shining brighter and brighter in the military sphere, and alas, too, to set before it had reached its zenith. Following in his wake, ever ready to stand by you in the hour of danger, to share with you your toils and hardships, to cheer you on in the hour of conflict, following strictly in the footsteps of his illustrious predecessor, the champion of your rights and reputation came your second Colonel—Owen Jones.

Officers and Soldiers—through your esteem I had the honor to be your next commander, and as such I deem it an high honor to-day to stand before the shattered remnant of what was once a large regiment. To thank you for your esteem and the willingness with which you have acceded to my every request, and complied with my every command, and for the manner you have so nobly and faithfully discharged your duties as soldiers. I believe I am the only officer now left of those who were assembled at the call of the Governor, and witnessed the organization of the regiment in the presence of his staff, and heard it christened the First Pennsylvania Reserve Cavalry; and it gives me pleasure to-day, to think we can return to our native State, those colors entrusted to our care, tattered and torn though they be, without a tarnish or a stain upon the reputation of the regiment.

Officers and Soldiers of the First Pennsylvania Reserve Cavalry, you are the veterans of more than thirty engagements, your banner has proudly floated over almost every field on which this historic army has been engaged; the graves of your comrades are strewn from Gettysburg to the river James; your war-path may be traced by the blood of your fallen heroes; but by the strength of justice and the might of mercy you have plumed your arms with honor and victory.

Enlisted veterans:—When you were re-enlisting my lips were sealed from encouraging you, because circumstances unavoidable, rendered my remaining with you impossible; let not our leaving discourage you, but go on to greater deeds of valor; be faithful, be obedient, be prompt and cheerful in duty as you always have been, a hopeful country awaits to crown you; and we shall not forget you; we shall continue to breathe the desired hope and christian prayer that you may soon be permitted to return to your homes, when the red-handed monster, *war*—whose pestiferous breath blasts with withering death every thing lovely on earth—may be banished from our distracted land, and peace, sweet peace again returning, shed evermore her Heaven-born blessings on our fair Columbia's soil.

LETTER FROM BRIGADIER-GENERAL GREGG, ON THE DEPARTURE OF THE REGIMENT FROM THE DIVISION FOR HOME.

Headquarters, Second Division Cavalry Corps, A. O. P.,
Sept. 1st, 1864.

COLONEL J. P. TAYLOR,

First Penna. Res. Cavalry.

MY DEAR COLONEL:—The order discharging from the United States' service the First Pennsylvania Cavalry, has been received at these Headquarters. As you will accompany your regiment to Pennsylvania, there to be discharged with it, I cannot permit your departure without expressing to you how much I feel the separation of yourself and command from the Second Division.

For nearly two years the First Pennsylvania Reserve Cavalry has been under my command, and now, at the end of its term of service, I can proudly say *its record is without a blemish.*

The excellence of your regiment resulted from the proper application of discipline by its officers. In the many engagements of this division, in which your regiment has participated, many officers and enlisted men have fallen. *They met death facing the foe,* let them be properly remembered by those who survive.

To you, Colonel, my thanks are due, for the efficient manner in which you have always performed your duty, whether as a regimental or brigade commander. You return to your home well satisfied that you have failed not in your duty, bearing with you the sincere friendship of myself and all your companions in arms.

With the very best wishes for your health, happiness and success in the future.

I am very truly yours,

D. McM. GREGG,

Brig.-Gen. Comd'g Second Cav. Div.

RECORD OF BATTLES,

IN WHICH THE REGIMENT HAS BEEN ENGAGED.

DRAINESVILLE, VA., December 20, 1861, advance skirmishers and supporting batteries.

HARRISONBURG, June 6, 1862, supporting Bucktails.

CROSS KEYS, June 8, 1862, rear guard and supporting batteries.

CEDAR MOUNTAIN, August 9, 1862, supporting battery and skirmishing—grand charge of first battalion, one hundred and sixteen men against a division of the enemy.

GAINESVILLE, August 28, 1862, flanking and skirmishing to the front.

BULL RUN, first day, August 29, 1862, advance skirmishing and flanking.

BULL RUN, second day, August 30, 1862, flanking.

FREDERICKSBURG, December 13, 1862, advance skirmishing to left grand division.

BRANDY STATION, June 9, 1863, engaged with Stuart's Cavalry Corps.

ALDIE, June 21 and 22, 1863, Stuart's Cavalry.

GETTYSBURG, PA., July 2 and 3, 1863, stationed in rear of the left centre.

11*

SHEPHERDSTOWN, VA., July 16, 1863—a force of the enemy's infantry, cavalry and artillery.

CULPEPPER, September 13, 1863—enemy's cavalry.

AUBURN, October 14, 1863—advance of Lee's army, infantry, cavalry and artillery.

NEW HOPE CHURCH, December 27, 1863—advance of Ewell's Corps, infantry, cavalry and artillery.

TODD'S TAVERN, May 5 and 6, 1864—against the enemy's cavalry corps.

CHILDSBURG, May 9, 1864—enemy's cavalry.

RICHMOND HEIGHTS and MEADOW BRIDGE, May 12, 1864—artillery, infantry and cavalry.

HAWS' SHOP, May 28, 1864—rebel cavalry corps and mounted infantry.

COLD HARBOR, June 1, 1864, but slightly engaged.

BARKER'S MILL, June 2, 1864—enemy's artillery and infantry.

TREVILLIAN STATION, June 12, 1864—cavalry, infantry and artillery.

WHITE HOUSE, June 21, 1864—cavalry and artillery.

ST. MARY'S CHURCH, June 24, 1864—enemy's cavalry corps.

MALVERN HILL, July 28, 1864—division of rebel infantry.

LEE'S MILLS, July 31, 1864—Butler's rebel cavalry.

GRAVEL HILL, August 14, 1864—cavalry, infantry and artillery.

REAM'S STATION, August 25, 1864—Hill's rebel corps.

LIST OF SKIRMISHES,

IN WHICH THE REGIMENT HAS BEEN ENGAGED.

Drainesville, November 27, 1861—guerrillas.

Falmouth, April 17 and 18, 1862—infantry and cavalry.

Gray's Farm, May 10, 1862—infantry pickets along the Rappahannock.

Strasburg, June 1; *Woodstock*, June 2; *Edinburg*, June 3.

Mt. Jackson, June 4; *New Market*, June 5, 1862—engaged with Jackson's rear guard, infantry, cavalry and artillery.

Rapidann River, August 3 and 4, 1862—infantry and cavalry.

Robinson River, August 8, 1862—advance of Jackson's army, infantry, cavalry and artillery.

Rappahannock Station, August 20, 1862—Stuart's cavalry.

At the several Fords along the Rappahannock, from the 20th to the 26th, 1862—repulsing the enemy in attempting to cross—infantry, cavalry and artillery.

Centreville, September 1, 1862—flank of Longstreet's army.

Fairfax Court House, September 2, 1862—flank of Longstreet's army.

Middleburg, October 30; *Aldie*, October 31, 1862—infantry, cavalry and artillery.

Salem, November 4, 1862—cavalry.

Warrenton, November 6—cavalry and artillery.

Rappahannock Bridge, November 7, 1862—cavalry and artillery.

Fredericksburg, December 12, 1862—left wing of Jackson's army.

Below Port Conway, April 22, 1863, Colonel Taylor and escort fired on by guerrillas, and three men killed.

Companies A and B, as advance for Sixth Corps, from Gettysburg to Hagerstown, five successive days.

Near Hazel River, August 4, 1863—cavalry.

Muddy River, August 6, 1863—cavalry.

Carter's Creek, September 6, 1863—picket reserve attacked by guerrillas. Lieutenant Lyon and Corporal Barre killed.

Along the Rappahannock, with little intermission, from September 14 to 20, 1863.

Sulphur Springs, October 12, 1863—cavalry and artillery.

Near Warrenton, November 17, 1863—picket reserve attacked.

Culpepper Ford, December 2, 1863.

Ashby's Gap, February 17, 1864—Moseby's guerrillas.

Charlotteville—while on a raid with General Custar.

Salem, March 19, 1864—Moseby's guerrillas.

Gravel Hill, August 16 and 17—enemy's cavalry.

Ream's Station, August 21, 22 and 23—cavalry and infantry.

RECORD OF MARCHES AND SCOUTS,

WITH APPROXIMATE DISTANCES TRAVELED.

August and September, 1861—in camp, near Washington, D. C.

October 10, 1861, moved to Langley, Va., a distance of eight miles.

19, 20 and 21, toward Leesburg, with advance of McCall's Division,, the Pennsylvania Reserve Corps, and return, thirty-two miles.

Total for October, 40 miles.

November 27, scout to Drainesville and beyond, thirty-six miles

Total for November, 36 miles.

December 20, to Drainesville, twenty-eight miles.

Total, for December, 28 miles.

January, 1862, two scouts beyond Difficult creek, twenty miles each.

Total for January, 40 miles.

February, a scout of twenty-five miles.

March 10, marched to Hunter's Mills, fourteen miles.

13, extensive scout toward Leesburg, forty-eight miles.

13 and .14, to near Alexandria, twenty-five miles.

15, to Falls Church, six miles.

Total for March, 94 miles.

April 9, To Fairfax Court House, ten miles.

April 10, to Manassas Junction, twenty miles.

11, to Catletts Station, twelve miles.

13 and 14, a scout to Hackett's Mills, near Safford Court House, twenty-five miles.

17 and 18 to Falmouth, thirty-five miles.

18 and 19, Companies G and H scout to Aquia Landing, thirty miles.

24 and 25, regiment sent to King George Court House, forty miles.

march, to camp, below Falmouth, six miles.

Total for April, 178 miles.

May 25, 1862, from six miles below Falmouth—beyond the Pamunkey river, toward Richmond.

28, return to Fredericksburg, about one hundred miles.

29, by way of Catletts Station to Strasburg, sixty miles.

Total for May, 160 miles.

June 1, Strasburg up the Shenandoah Valley, reaching Port Republic on the 9th, sixty miles.

9, back to Mt. Jackson, to Strasburg, reaching Manassas on the 23d.

Total for June, 155 miles.

July 4, marched to Warrenton Junction and famous scouts to the Rappahannock by portions of the regiment, ninety miles.

16, to Culpepper, twenty-five miles.

17, to Ragged Mountain fifteen miles, and scouting while there, forty-five miles.

22, returned to Culpepper, fifteen miles.

Total for July, 175 miles.

August 1, marched to Rapidann, fourteen miles.
Scouting by detachments for six days, one hundred miles.
8, to Cedar Mountain, eight miles.
20, to Rappahannock Station, twenty miles.
21, by a circuitous route, with numerous countermarches to Centreville, seventy miles.
Total for August, 212 miles.

September 1, to Alexandria, twenty-five miles.
3, to Bailey's Cross Roads, six miles.
26, detachment of five companies to Centreville, employed for four weeks in scouting Manassas plains, two hundred and fifty miles.
Total for September, 281 miles.

October 10, scout to Bealton Station and return, one hundred miles.
27 and 28, to Chantilly, twenty miles.
30, to Aldie, thirty miles.
Total for October, 150 miles.

November 1, return to Chantilly, twenty-five miles.
3, 4 and 5, to Upperville, thirty-seven miles.
6, by a circuitous route to Warrenton, twenty-five miles.
7, to Rappahannock Bridge, twelve miles.
20, 21 and 22, to Brook's Station, thirty-eight miles.
Total for November, 167 miles.

December 10, marched to Falmouth, ten miles.
14, to Lamb's Creek Church, ten miles.
28, to Bell Plain Landing, fourteen miles.
Total for December, 34 miles.

January 2, 1863, to picket at Lamb's Creek Church, ten miles.

5, return to Bell Plain Landing, ten miles.

8, to picket and return, twenty miles.

17, to picket and return, twenty miles.

21 to 23, Burnside's advance, twelve miles.

27, to picket and return, twenty miles.

Total for January, 92 miles.

February 2, to picket and return the 5th, twenty miles.

14, to picket and return the 17th, twenty miles.

27, to picket for ten days, ten miles.

Total for February, 50 miles.

March 5, relieved from picket and return to camp, ten miles.

19, to picket and return on the 19th, twenty miles; and scout at night to the neck below, forty miles.

21, another scout by detachment, forty miles.

Total for March, 110 miles.

April 12, to King George Court House, sixteen miles; scouts while on picket, seventy miles.

Total for April, 86 miles.

May 9, march to Potomac Creek Bridge, thirty miles.

18, to United States Ford, nine miles.

28, to Warrenton Junction, Morrisville and Bealton Station, thirty-five miles.

Total for May, 74 miles.

June, 1863, moved to Morrisville, fourteen miles.

9, to Brandy Station and returned to Rappahannock Station, eighteen miles.

10, to Warrenton Junction, twelve miles.

13, to Warrenton, nine miles.

June 15, to Manasas Junction, twenty miles.
16 and 17, to Aldie, twenty miles.
18, to Thoroughfare Gap, eight miles.
21 and 22, to Aldie and Upperville and return, thirty-two miles.
26, to Leesburg, nine miles.
27, crossed Edwards' Ferry and marched all night, reaching Frederick city next day.
29, to Middleburg, marching all night.
30, to Taneytown; total from the 27th, sixty miles.

Total for June, 202 miles.

July 1, to battle-field of Gettysburg, twelve miles.
5, to Creagarstown, twenty-five miles.
7, *via* Frederick city to Middleburg and South Mountain, twenty-two miles.
9, to Boonsboro', ten miles.
11, to Antietam Creek, five miles.
12, back to Boonsboro', five miles.
14, to Harper's Ferry, twenty-seven miles.
15, to Shepherdstown, Va., and return the night of the 16th to Harper's Ferry, eighteen miles.
19, crossed the Shenandoah river east, six miles.
20, to Perryville, ten miles.
21, to Hillsboro', four miles.
23, to Ashby's Gap, twenty miles.
26, move through Upperville to Middleburg, fourteen miles.
27, through White Plains to Warrenton, twenty miles.

July 28, to Warrenton Junction, nine miles.
29, to Warrenton, nine miles.
30, to Amisville, south of Rappahannock, fifteen miles.
Total for July, 232 miles.

August 4, scout toward Culpepper, sixteen miles.
5, scout toward Culpepper, sixteen miles.
8, return to Sulphur Springs and on picket, eight miles.
15, to Warrenton, six miles.
18, scout by detachment to Salem and returned, eighteen miles.
19, scout to Gainesville and return, forty miles.
24, crossed the Rappahannock to Jefferson on picket and returned on 27th, eighteen miles.
Total for August, 112 miles.

September 4, on picket at Carter's Creek, eight miles.
7, return to camp, eight miles.
10 and 11; scout to Middleburg and return, fifty miles.
12, to Jefferson, eight miles.
13, through Culpepper to Cedar Mountain, twenty-seven miles.
14, to the Rapidann, five miles.
18, return to Culpepper, eleven miles.
22, to the Rapidann, eight miles.
25, to Culpepper, eight miles.
26, moved back to Catletts Station, seventeen miles; scouting while here, 50 miles.
Total for September, 205 miles.

October 3, to United States Ford, a circuitous route, forty miles.

October 11, to Rappahannock Station, twenty-five miles.
13, to Auburn, ten miles.
14, to Brentsville, ten miles.
15, crossed and re-crossed Bull Run, twenty miles; picket and scout along Bull Run, twenty miles.
21, move to Gainesville, twelve miles.
22, to Warrenton, twelve miles.
Total for October, 149 miles.

November 6, move to Bealton Station, twelve miles.
9, to Fayetteville, nine miles.
21, pursuit of Moseby, thirty miles.
23, marched to Bealton Station, nine miles.
24, beyond the Rappahannock, eighteen miles.
26, cross the Rapidann and in the direction of Orange Court House, twenty-five miles.
27, to battle-field of New Hope Church and return to Parker's Store, twenty-five miles.
28, to Wilderness Tavern and return to Parker's Store on 30th, fifteen miles.
Total for November, 143 miles.

December 1, to Wilderness Tavern, seven miles.
2, re-crossed the Rapidann, fourteen miles.
6, to Brandy Station, twelve miles.
10 and 11, to Warrenton for winter quarters, twenty-two miles.
25, scout by detachment to Salem and return, eighteen miles.
Total for December, 73 miles.

January 1, 1864, to Front Royal and return on the 4th, seventy miles.

January 8, to Salem and return, eighteen miles.
Total for January, 88 miles.

February 17, scout to Ashby's Gap and return, sixty miles.
27, to Charlotteville and return, seventy-eight miles.
Total for February, 138 miles.

March 7, to New Baltimore and return, ten miles.
8, to Sulphur Springs and return, ten miles; various scouts during the month, one hundred and thirty miles.
Total for March, 150 miles.

April 21, to Turkey Run, six miles.
24, to Morrisville, eighteen miles.
Total for April 24 miles.

May 3, to Richardsville, eighteen miles.
4, to Pine Creek, ten miles.
5 to 8, marching and counter-marching, thirty miles.
9 to 14, marched *via* Fredericksburg, Childsburg, North Anna, Beaverdam Station, South Anna, at Ground Squirrel bridge, Hungary Station, Brock road, Meadow bridge, Bottom bridge to James river, at Haxall's Landing, ninety miles.
17 to 25, *via* Jordon's bridge, Baltimore Cross Roads, Cold Harbor, White House, Ayletts, White Chimneys to Chesterfield Station, one hundred and ten miles.
26 to June 3, *via* Pamunky, at Hanovertown, Haws' Shop, Cold Harbor, marching and counter-marching to Bottom bridge, sixty miles.

June 6 to 25, from Bottom bridge *via* New Castle, crossing the Pamunky at that place, Ayletts, Pole Cat Station, crossed North East river and North Anna River to Trevillian Station, and returned *via* the Catharpen road, Spottsylvania Court House, Guinea Station, Bowling Green, Newtown, Clarksville, Walkertown, King and Queen Court House, and returned to Clarksville, crossed Matapony river at Dunkirk, and again *via* Ayletts, King William Court House to White House, and then to James river at Wyandott's Landing, one hundred and eighty-three miles.

27 of June to 4th of July, 20 miles.

July 11 to 16, to Jerusalem Plank road, Reams Station and return, forty-eight miles.

25 to *August* 8, crossing the James river to Malvern Hill and return *via* Reams Station to Light House Point, fifty-eight miles.

11 to 13, to Jerusalem Plank road and return, thirty miles.

From night of 13th to *September* 1, across the James river, back to army headquarters, to Weldon Railroad and return to City Point, sixty-five miles.

Total from May to September, 672 miles.

Total for 1861, 112 miles.

Total for 1862, 1631 miles.

Total for 1863, 1528 miles.

Total for 1864, 1068 miles.

Sum total for three years 4339 miles

COMMISSIONED OFFICERS.

By the law of the Pennsylvania Reserve Corps, company officers were elected by the men of their respective companies, and the commanding and field officers were elected by the commissioned officers of the regiment. This mode of choosing has not been productive of so many evil results in this regiment as in many others, but it is plainly evident from experience, that a faithful performance of duty is incompatible with attempts to secure popularity among his subordinates, on the part of either commissioned or non-commissioned officers, who are seeking promotion by the votes of those under their command; consequently those who have best filled subordinate posts, are least likely to secure promotion by election. This system was annulled by an Act of Legislature, early in 1863, and since then the officers have been appointed in the manner presented by the military laws of the State of Pennsylvania.

FIELD OFFICERS.

Colonels.

George D. Bayard, commissioned August 1, 1861; appointed brigadier-general, May 5, 1862. Killed at Fredericksburg, December 13, 1862.

Owen Jones, commissioned May 5, 1862, and resigned January 30, 1863,

J. P. Taylor, commissioned January 30, 1863; commanding First Brigade, Second Cavalry Division, since October 8, 1863.

Lieutenant-Colonels.

Jacob Higgins, commissioned August 1, 1861, and resigned October 8, 1861.

Owen Jones, commissioned October, 1861. Promoted to colonel.

S. D. Barrows, commissioned May 5, 1862. Resigned for disability, September, 1862.

J. P. Taylor, commissioned September, 1862. Promoted to colonel.

David Gardner, commissioned February 10, 1863. Commanding regiment since October, 1863, and part of the time, brigade.

Majors.

Owen Jones, commissioned August, 1861. Promoted to lieutenant-colonel

S. D. Barrows, commissioned October, 1861. Promoted to lieutenant-colonel.

R. J. Falls, commissioned January 3, 1862. Wounded July 28, 1864; transferred to First Pennsylvania Veteran Cavalry Battalion.

Thomas J. Richards, commissioned May 5, 1862, and resigned for disability.

J. H. Ray, commissioned May 5, 1862, and resigned for disability, February 23, 1863.

Wm. T. McEwen, commissioned February 23, 1863, and resigned for disability October 17, 1863. Wounded at Brandy Station, June 9, 1863.

David Gardner, commissioned November 23, 1862. Promoted to lieutenant-colonel.

James M. Gaston, commissioned February 12, 1863. On detached service at headquarters, Second Cavalry Division, since June, 1863.

STAFF OFFICERS.

Adjutants.

Charles C. Townsend, commissioned November 22, 1862, and resigned for disability June 14, 1863.

Wm. P. Llŏyd, commissioned June 16, 1863.

Quarter Masters.

R. R. Corson, commissioned August, 1861. Promoted to brigade quarter-master.

George H. Baker, commissioned May 5, 1862.

Assistant Commissaries of Subsistence.

Wm. Stadelman, commissioned November 22, 1862, and resigned for disability, January 28, 1863.

Henry A. Wood, commissioned January 28, 1863.

MEDICAL DEPARTMENT.

Surgeons.

David Stanton, commissioned August, 1861, and promoted to the regular army, November 24, 1862.

G. B. Hotchkin, commissioned November 24, 1862. Acting surgeon-in-chief of First Brigade, Second Cavalry Division, greater part of the last year.

Assistant Surgeons.

Samuel Alexander, commissioned August, 1861, and was killed in a skirmish at Drainesville, Virginia, November 27, 1861.

G. B. Hotchkin, commissioned November 27, 1861. Promoted to surgeon.

L. E. Atkinson, commissioned January 21, 1863.

H. N. Kelly, commissioned December, 1862. Resigned for disability.

R. H. Tuft, commissioned July 29, 1863.

J. B. Finney, commissioned August, 1861. Resigned September, 1861.

S. W. H. Calver, commissioned June, 1862. Resigned August 2, 1862.

Chaplain.

J. Hervey Beale, commissioned September 16, 1861.

Battalion Adjutants.

C. L. Buffington, commissioned March 1, 1862; and mustered out of service, in pursuance of an Act of Congress, annulling the office, September, 1862.

Wm. S. Foster, commissioned March 1, 1862; and mustered out of service, in pursuance of an Act of Congress, annulling the office, September, 1862.

Job H. Cole, commissioned March 1, 1862; and mustered out of service, in pursuance of an Act of Congress, annulling the office, September, 1862.

LINE OFFICERS.—A COMPANY.

Captains.

John K. Robinson, commissioned July 29, 1861, and resigned March 28, 1862.

Thomas J. Frow, commissioned March 28, 1862, and resigned March 14, 1863.

Wm. H. Patterson, commissioned March 28, 1863.

First Lieutenants.

Thomas J. Frow, commissioned July 29, 1861. Promoted to captain.

Wm. H. Patterson, commissioned March 28, 1862. Promoted to captain.

James R. Kelly, commissioned March 8, 1863. Wounded July 17, 1863. Prisoner June 24, 1864.

Second Lieutenants.

Wm. H. Patterson, commissioned July 29, 1861. Promoted to first lieutenant.

James R. Kelly, commissioned March 28, 1862. Promoted to first lieutenant.

D. H. Wilson, commissioned March 28, 1863. Killed June 2, 1864.

B COMPANY.

Captains.

Jacob Stadelman, commissioned August 8, 1861. Resigned March 26, 1862.

Joseph C. Roberts, commissioned March 26, 1862. Resigned May 8, 1862.

Wm. Litzenberg, commissioned May 8, 1862. Wounded July 28, 1864.

First Lieutenants.

Theodore Streck, commissioned August 8, 1861. Promoted to captain, Company H, November 26, 1861; wounded February, 1862.

John Kline, commissioned November 25, 1861. Resigned December 30, 1861.

Joseph C. Roberts, commissioned January 1, 1862. Promoted to captain.

William Buzby, commissioned March 26, 1862. Died March, 1864.

Second Lieutenants.

John Kline, commissioned August 8, 1861. Promoted to first lieutenant.

Joseph C. Roberts, commissioned November 25, 1861. Promoted to first lieutenant.

William Buzby, commissioned January 3, 1862. Promoted to first lieutenant.

Robert S. Lawsha, commissioned March 26, 1862. Wounded May 28, 1864. Promoted to first lieutenant.

C COMPANY.

Captains.

J. P. Taylor, commissioned August 6, 1861. Promoted to lieutenant-colonel.

William T. McEwen, commissioned October, 1862. Promoted to major.

R. J. McNitt, commissioned February 13, 1863. Prisoner June 21, 1864.

First Lieutenants.

William Mann, commissioned August, 1861. Resigned February 26, 1862.

William T. McEwen, commissioned February 26, 1862. Promoted captain.

R. J. McNitt, commissioned October, 1862. Promoted to captain.

Hiram McClenahen, commissioned February 12, 1863. Wounded July 17, 1863; absent on recruiting service since August, 1863.

Second Lieutenants.

William T. McEwen, commissioned August, 1861. Promoted to first lieutenant.

R. J. McNitt, commissioned February 26, 1862. Promoted to first lieutenant.

John W. Nelson, commissioned October, 1862. Transferred to First Pennsylvania Veteran Cavalry Battalion, September 1, 1864.

D COMPANY.

Captains.

J. W. Smith, commissioned August, 1861. Resigned September, 1861.

William S. Gile, commissioned September 20, 1861. Resigned June 24, 1862.

Hugh A. McDonald, commissioned July 1, 1862, was wounded in three different places in the battle of Cedar Mountain, August 9, 1862.

First Lieutenants.

S. D. Barrows, commissioned August 1, 1861. Promoted to major.

Warren L. Holbrook, commissioned July 1, 1862; transferred to First Pennsylvania Veteran Cavalry Battalion, September 1, 1864.

Second Lieutenants.

M. L. French, commissioned November 15, 1862. Promoted to Captain of Company E.

William F. Butcher, commissioned July 1, 1862; killed in action at Cedar Mountain, August 9, 1862.

Philip H. Walker, commissioned September 9, 1862. Resigned for disability February 23, 1864, S. O. No. 52.

A. R. McDonald, promoted July, 1864; veteran volunteer.

E COMPANY.

Captains.

Jonathan Wolf, commissioned August, 1, 1861. Resigned November, 1861.

Robert R. Lipton, commissioned November, 1861. Resigned April, 1862.

Jeremiah Newman, commissioned February, 1863.

First Lieutenants.

Robert R. Lipton, commissioned August, 1861. Promoted to captain.

John A. Bayard, commissioned November, 1861. Resigned February, 1862.

Jeremiah Newman, commissioned April, 1862. Promoted to captain.

William P. Lloyd, commissioned March 22, 1863. Promoted to adjutant.

Samuel Lipton, commissioned February 10, 1863. Resigned for disability March 2, 1863.

Johnston C. Akers, commissioned June 16, 1863.

Second Lieutenants.

Samuel Murray, commissioned August 1, 1861. Resigned December, 1861.

Samuel Deavenport, commissioned December, 1862. Resigned March, 1862.

Samuel Lipton, commissioned May, 1862. Promoted to first lieutenant.

Amos M. Herrick, commissioned February 11, 1861. Transferred to First Pennsylvania Veteran Cavalry Battalion September 1, 1864.

F COMPANY.

Captains.

J. M. Harper, commissioned August 15, 1861. Resigned October 19, 1861.

J. H. Ray, commissioned November 15, 1861. Promoted to major.

Alexander Davidson, commissioned April 1, 1862. Died of wounds July 31, 1864.

First Lieutenants.

J. H. Ray, commissioned August 15, 1861. Promoted to captain.

Alexander Davidson, commissioned November 15, 1861. Promoted to captain.

Lewis K. Evans, commissioned January 13, 1862. Resigned June 22, 1862.

Thomas Lucas, commissioned August 17, 1862. Received a sabre wound from the enemy June 9, 1863. Promoted to captain.

Second Lieutenants.

Alexander Davidson, commissioned August, 1861. Promoted to first lieutenant.

Lewis K. Evans, commissioned November 15, 1861. Promoted to first lieutenant.

Samuel Greenlee, commissioned June 13, 1862 Wounded June 9, 1863, killed May 28, 1864.

G COMPANY.

Captains.

Jacob Higgins, commissioned August, 1861. Promoted to lieutenant-colonel.

David Gardner, commissioned August, 1861. Promoted to major.

Henry C. Beamer, commissioned November, 1862. Resigned for disability April 12, 1863.

Francis P. Confer, commissioned April 12, 1863.

First Lieutenants.

David Gardner, commissioned August, 1861. Promoted to captain.

Hampton S. Thomas, commissioned September, 1861. Promoted to Captain of Company M.

Henry C. Beamer, commissioned April, 1862. Promoted to captain November 24, 1864.

Francis P. Confer, commissioned November 24, 1862. Promoted to captain.

Alonzo Reed, commissioned November 24, 1862. Killed June 24, 1864.

Hiram Platt, commissioned, August 1, 1864. First Pennsylvania Veteran Cavalry Battalion.

Second Lieutenants.

Hampton S. Thomas, commissioned August, 1761. Promoted to first lieutenant

H. C. Weir, commissioned November, 1861. Promoted to captain and A. A. G. on General Bayard's staff.

Francis P. Confer, commissioned November, 1862. Promoted to first lieutenant.

Alonzo Reed, commissioned November 24, 1862. Promoted to first lieutenant.

George J. Geiser, commissioned April 12, 1863. Dismissed, February 17, 1864.

H COMPANY.

Captains.

James B. Davidson, commissioned August, 1861. Resigned September, 1861.

Theodore Streck, commissioned November 24, 1861. Resigned December, 1862. Wounded May 24, 1862.

William S. Craft, commissioned February 12, 1863. Wounded May 28, 1864.

First Lieutenants.

David Gilmore, commissioned August, 1861. Resigned November, 1861.

John D. Scott, commissioned November 21, 1861. Dismissed September, 1862.

William S. Craft, commissioned September 12, 1862. Promoted to captain.

Thomas C. Labo, commissioned February 12, 1862. Wounded July 28, 1864; transferred to First Pennsylvania Veteran Cavalry Battalion, September 1, 1864.

Second Lieutenants.

William Brown, commissioned August, 1861. Resigned October 8, 1861.

James Jackson, commissioned September, 1861. Resigned November, 1861.

Thomas C. Lebo, commissioned November, 1861. Promoted to first lieutenant.

Eli C. Forsyth, commissioned February 12, 1863.

I COMPANY.

Captains.

W. W. McNulty, commissioned August 13, 1861. Resigned.

John W Ross, commissioned August 24, 1861. Resigned November 22, 1861

George T. Work, commissioned August 23, 1861. Resigned.

James M. Gaston, commissioned July 12, 1862. Promoted to major February 10, 1863.

T. C. McGregor, commissioned February 26, 1863. Transferred to First Pennsylvania Veteran Cavalry Battalion, September 1, 1864.

First Lieutenants.

John W. Ross, commissioned August, 1861. Promoted to captain.

George T. Work, commissioned August, 1861. Promoted to captain.

James M. Gaston, commissioned November 23, 1861. Promoted to captain.

T. C. McGregor, commissoned July 12, 1862. Promoted to captain.

F. S. Morgan, commissioned February 12, 1863. Transferred to First Pennsylvania Veteran Cavalry Battalion September 1, 1864.

Second Lieutenants.

George W. Seigrist, commissioned November 23, 1861. Resigned May 10, 1862.

J. B. Richey, commissioned July 12, 1862. Dismissed February 18, 1863.

J. M. Gaston, commissioned August 1, 1861. Promoted to first lieutenant.

T. C. McGregor, commissioned May 10, 1862. Promoted to first lieutenant.

George W. Lyon, commissioned February 25, 1863. Killed in action by guerrillas September 6, 1863.

K COMPANY.

Captains.

William Boyce, commissioned September, 1861. Resigned December 17, 1861.

J. H. Williams, commissioned January 5, 1862. Dismissed February 3, 1864; reinstated May, 1864, and transferred to First Pennsylvania Veteran Cavalry Battalion September 1, 1864.

First Lieutenants.

William A. Kennedy, commissioned September, 1861. Wounded May 28, 1864.

Second Lieutenants.

Samuel W. Morgan, commissioned September, 1861. Wounded September 15, 1863.

L COMPANY.

Captains.

J. C. A. Hoffeditz, commissioned August, 1861. Resigned April 16, 1862.

Wm. A. Sands, commissioned April 16, 1862. Prisoner June 21, 1864.

First Lieutenants.

Wm. A. Sands, commissioned August 1, 1861. Promoted to captain.

H. S. Gaul, commissioned April 16, 1862.

Second Lieutenants.

H. S. Gaul, commissioned August, 1861. Promoted to first lieutenant.

Charles Lichtenthaller, commissioned April 19, 1862. Resigned June 26, 1863.

David S. Buxton, commissioned June 26, 1863. Wounded December 27, 1863; mortally wounded and prisoner, June 21, 1864.

M COMPANY.

Captains.

Thomas S. Richards, commissioned August, 1861. Promoted to major.

H. S. Thomas, commissioned May 5, 1862. Detached as A. A. Inspector-general First Brigade, since April, 1863. Transferred to First Pennsylvania Veteran Cavalry Battalion.

First Lieutenants.

George D. Leaf, commissioned August, 1861. Resigned January, 1863.

Henderson Sample, commissioned February 12, 1863. Resigned August 12, 1864.

Second Lieutenants.

A. S. Shollenberger, commissioned August, 1861. Resigned.

Henderson Sample, commissioned December 30, 1861. Promoted to first lieutenant.

Joseph S. Wright, commissioned February 12, 1863. Mortally wounded, June 24, 1864.

NON-COMMISSIONED STAFF.

Sergeant Majors.

George W. Seigrist, appointed September 28, 1861. Promoted to second lieutenant.

C. L. Buffington, appointed November 23, 1861. Promoted to battalion adjutant.

Henry C. Beamer, appointed February 17, 1862. Promoted to first lieutenant.

Wm. McEwen, appointed May 8, 1862. Discharged for disability, September 29, 1862.

George J. Geiser, appointed September 29, 1862. Promoted to second lieutenant.

John Hamilton, appointed April 12, 1863.

Quartermaster Sergeants.

George H. Baker, appointed September 28, 1861. Promoted to quartermaster.

Wm. Stadelman, appointed May 5, 1862. Promoted to A. C. S.

George W. Fincher, appointed October 28, 1862. Vet. vol , February 1, 1864.

Commissary Sergeants.

Henry A. Wood, appointed June 5, 1862. Promoted to A. C. S.

John McCahan, appointed January 27, 1863.

Chief Buglers.

Thomas R. Storer, appointed October 16, 1861. Mustered out, in pursuance of an Act of Congress, annulling the office, September, 1862.

James P. Landis, appointed May 1, 1863. Wounded June 9, 1863. Vet. vol., February 1, 1864.

Hospital Stewards.

Joseph Deveney, appointed September 6, 1861. Transferred.

C. C. Townsend, appointed September, 1861. Promoted to adjutant.

Ernest Conzler, appointed October, 1861. Transferred to regular army November, 1862.

Charles Gardner, appointed October, 1862.

Wm. P. Lloyd, appointed December 18, 1862. Promoted to first lieutenant.

William J. Jackman, appointed March 22, 1863.

Regimental Veterinary Surgeon.

Jacob Woolf, appointed July, 1863.

ORGANIZATION OF A COMPANY, FIRST PENNSYLVANIA RESERVE CAVALRY.

Company A was recruited in Juniatta County, State of Pennsylvania, September, 1859, by Captain John H. Patterson, and was called the "Juniatta Cavalry."

On the 16th day of April, 1861, the company was re-organized and recruited by Lieutenant John K. Robison, and ordered by the Governor of Pennsylvania to be in readiness to report to Harrisburg at short notice.

On the 25th day of July, 1861, the company was reorganized again, by the election of Lieutenant Robison, captain, T. J. Frow, first lieutenant and Wm. H. Patterson, second lieutenant. On the 26th of the same month it reported to Harrisburg, and was accepted, and on the first day of August, 1861, was mustered into the State service by Colonel Taggart, for three years.

On the 16th day of August, 1861, it was assigned to the regiment, and ordered to report to Washington, D. C., and was mustered into the United States service, on the 27th, at Camp Jones, near Washington, where it joined the regiment.

ENLISTED MEN OF A COMPANY.

John H. Fertig, orderly sergeant. Prisoner June 21, 1864.

W. S. Miller, quartermaster sergeant. Wounded at White House, June 21, 1864.

S. L. Patterson, commissary sergeant.

L. R. Beale, first duty sergeant.

S. S. Wilson, second duty sergeant.

J. T. Funk, third duty sergeant. Wounded June 24, 1864.

S. F. Lane, fourth duty sergeant. Transferred to Signal Corps.

J. T. Sterret, fifth duty sergeant.

W. A. Patterson, first corporal. Prisoner, June 21, 1864.

S. S. Mairs, second corporal. Vet. vol., January 1, 1864. Prisoner, June 21, 1864.

D. Snyder, third corporal.

J. Q. Eby, fourth corporal. Prisoner June 21, 1864.

Wm. Bortle, fifth corporal.

Brazee, John M.

Bear, W. A. Wounded at White House, June 21, 1864.

Berkey, Elijah

Baird, James

Bidler, Henry W.

Brown, W. M.

Bortle, Henry

Birchfield, James M. Vet. vol., February 1, 1864.

Berkyhiser, Isaac

Collier, David W.

Campbell, Noah, bugler. Vet. vol., January 1, 1864.
Doty, John E., corporal. Wounded June 24, 1864.
Ernest, Wesley H.
Fink, George. Wounded at Culpepper, September 15, 1863, and wounded July 28, 1864.
Folly, James
Fulton, Wm. S. Wounded in Pennsylvania, July 10, 1863.
Folly, Michael
Horton, Daniel T. Prisoner, April 18, 1863.
Hardee, John.
Hawler, Israel. Wounded October 1, 1863.
Hurshey, John.
Johns, Mathias. Vet. vol., January 1, 1864.
Kinsloe, Armstrong.
Kinsloe, John.
Kennedy, Joseph B. Vet. vol., January 1, 1864.
Longacre, Isaac. Prisoner at Bull Run, August 30, 1862.
Lowden, Alfred M.
Meloy, George W. Private Orderly to General Meade since enlistment.
McDonald, J. B.
McDonald, Anderson H.
McWilliams, Andrew J.
McCoy, John M.
Marly, James B.
McConnel, Henry O, bugler. Transferred to the Signal Corps, March, 1864.
Nicely, Henry. Vet. vol., January 1, 1864.
Nipple, John O. Wounded June 24, 1864.
Nicely, Jacob.

Okeson, Samuel B.
Rogers, Matthew H.
Riner, Jonathan.
Smith, W. H. Killed May 28, 1864, at Haws' Shop, Va.
Smith, David L.
Smith, William. Sent to Insane Asylum.
Sperry, William Vet. vol., January 1, 1864.
Wildman, Abraham J. Vet. vol. January 1, 1864. Wounded June 2, 1864.
Dunn, William. Vet. vol., January 1, 1864.
Marshman, Samuel.
Renor, Mattorck.
Slusher, J. K. P.
Logan, Thomas C.
Howard, Henry. Wounded June 21, 1864.
Robertson, Joseph. Wounded June 24, 1864.

PROMOTED.

John, Hamilton. Sergeant to sergeant-major, May 1, 1863.
John W. Forney. Sergeant to saddler sergeant, November, 1862. Vet. vol., February 1, 1864.
William J. Jackman. Sergeant to hospital steward, March 22, 1863.
James R. Kelly. Sergeant to second lieutenant, March 28, 1862.
D. H. Wilson. Sergeant to second lieutenant, March 25, 1863.

KILLED.

John Neiman. Culpepper, Va., September 13, 1863.

DIED.

Jacob Benson. Disease, September 12, 1861.

DISCHARGED.

Isaac Clair. Disability, February, 1863.
John Clair. Disability, March, 1863.
T. W. Dewess. Disability, March 24, 1862.
Smith De Bray. Disability, March 1, 1862.
Joseph R. Kinser. Disability, November 22, 1862.
James McKee. Disability, September 18, 1862.
Samuel M. Mitchell. Disability, May 12, 1862.
Geo. H. McCochron. Disability, May 1, 1862.
Alonzo Morley. Disability, April 1, 1862.
Newton Lane, sergeant. Disability, March, 1863.
W. M. Robinson. Wounded at Cedar Mountain, August 9, 1862.
Levi Richer. Disability, January 8, 1862.
Calvin E. Stewart. Disability.
John A. Tomey. Disability, January, 1862.
Amos Wolfgang, corporal. Disability, February, 1863.
Wm. Wagner, corporal. Disability, December, 1862.
Joseph Yocum. Disability, April 1, 1862.
David Holtzhopple, corporal. February, 1863, from wounds at Bull run, August 30, 1862.
Joseph G. Simpson. Disability, March, 1863.

TRANSFERRED.

Samuel Gazette. Invalid Corps.

DESERTED.

Alexander R. Brant. July 25, 1862.
John L. Ernest. September 1, 1861.
Christopher R. Richard.
G. W. Tannyhill. August 18, 1861.

ORGANIZATION OF B COMPANY, FIRST REGIMENT PENNSYLVANIA RESERVE CAVALRY.

B Company was organized at Athensville, Montgomery county, State of Pennsylvania, on or about the 22d day of April, 1861, by the Honorable Owen Jones, who was unanimously chosen captain. Dr. Joseph Levering was chosen first lieutenant, and Jacob L. Stadelman second lieutenant.

On the 5th day of August it was ordered to report at Harrisburg, Pennsylvania, where it arrived the same day, and encamped in Camp Curtin.

Dr. Joseph H. Levering, having resigned his lieutenantcy, previous to the company leaving Athensville, an election was held for the purpose of filling the vacancy, on the 6th day of August, 1861, when second lieutenant Jacob L. Stadelman was chosen first lieutenant, and John Kline, second lieutenant.

On the 8th day of August, 1861, the company was mustered into the State service, by Colonel Taggart, of the Twelfth regiment Pennsylvania Volunteer Reserve Corps.

Captain Owen Jones, having been promoted to the rank of major, First Lieutenant Jacob L. Stadelman was elected captain, and Theodore Streck was elected first lieutenant on the 16th of the same month.

On the same day, the company left Camp Curtin, and arrived at Washington, D. C., and encamped at the Park on Seventh street.

On the 20th day of August it moved to Camp Jones, and to Camp Reynolds, near Tennallytown on the 18th of September, 1861.

ENLISTED MEN OF B COMPANY.

John H. Bevan, orderly sergeant.
Adolphus S. Eder, first duty sergeant.
Martin Mars, second duty sergeant.
David W. Tarrence, third duty sergeant. Wounded, May 25, 1863.
Joseph Price, fourth duty sergeant.
Washington F. Chrissman, quartermaster sergeant. Wounded at Culpepper, September 13, 1863.
David W. Titlow, commissary sergeant.

John R Styer, first corporal. Killed May 28, 1864.
Geo. B. Rambo, second corporal.
Crawford Yocum, third corporal.
Kline A. Graver, fourth corporal.
Wm. H. Ramsey, fifth corporal
Joel L. Davis, sixth corporal.
Mark R. Hagner, seventh corporal.
Henry H. Pyott, eighth corporal.

Baxter, Amos
Bennett, Charles. Vet. vol., February 1, 1864.
Black, John. Vet. vol., February 1, 1864.
Black, Lorenzo D.
Bevan, Allen L.
Bisson, Jacob G.
Connell, Patrick. Wounded in Pennsylvania, July 5, 1863, and at Cold Harbor, June 1, 1864.
Collins, Edgar W.
Campbell, Flemming
Cornman, Joseph.
Creighton, John J. Vet. vol., February 1, 1864.

Davidson, Charles
Davis, Peter
Gregor, Chalkly F.
Hoffman, Thomas P.
Hampton, Wm. S.
Haws, Samuel A. Killed May 28, 1864.
Hafner, Mathias
Jago, Samuel. Vet. vol., February 1, 1864.
Jacobs, Enos.
Lowery, Robert. Vet. vol., February 1, 1864.
Levering, Perry H.
Lysle, George L. Sergeant. Vet. vol., February 1, 1864. Killed, July 28, 1864.
McFayne, James J.
Maiser, Connard
Michael, Matthew. Vet. vol., February 1, 1864.
Moore, Lewis. Wounded, July 28, 1864.
Matson, Morris M. Bugler.
Quinn, John
Rhoads, Wm. H.
Ritter, John
Snyder, Franklin. Bugler.
Smoyer, Edward B.
Soley, Wesley A.
Smith, Isaac W.
Smith, Joseph
Staub, Michael B.
Vaugn, Hamilton
Warnock, Edward
Yocum, John. Killed, May 28, 1864.
Bynn, Geo. W.
Haines, Jacob W.

Grant, John S.
Kramer, Charles
Blehl, Francis
Lutz, Justus W.
Moore, Joseph F. Wounded at Culpepper, September 13, 1863, also, June 2, 1864, at Barker's Mills.
Adair, William
Edler, William H Wounded, June 21, 1864.
Mower, Philip A. Mortally wounded, June 2, 1864.
Miles, John J.
Milan,, Thomas

PROMOTED.

Wm. Buzby. Sergeant to second lieutenant.
Geo. H. Baker. Sergeant to quartermaster, May 5, 1862.
R. R. Corson. Sergeant to quartermaster, September, 1861.
Rob't S. Lawsha. Sergeant to second lieutenant, April, 1862.
Wm. Litzenberg. Sergeant to captain, May 2, 1862.
Wm. Stadelman. Sergeant to A. C. S., November, 22, 1862.

KILLED.

Howard A. McAfee. At Auburn, Va., October 14, 1863.
John Smith. Killed at Auburn, Va., October 11, 1863.

DIED.

Rob't Maxwell. Disease, April 4, 1862.
Theodore, Shaeffer. Disease, October 18, 1861.

DISCHARGED.

Theodore F. Ashenfelter. Disability, February 26, 1863.

John F. Anderson. Corporal. Disability, October 9, 1861.

Wm. H. Bowden. Disability, 1862.

James Conard. Disability, 1862,

Elisha Davis. Disability, January 4, 1862.

Jacob H Detra. Disability, February 3, 1863.

Charles Ford. Disability, January 4, 1862.

Alexander Gotwaltz. Disability, March 20, 1863.

James McLennon. Disability, 1862.

Nathan Miller. Disability, January 4, 1862.

Washington Miller. Disability, January 4, 1862.

Lemuel A. Patterson. Sergeant. Disability, March 20, 1863.

Charles Quinby. Disability, January 20, 1862.

George Rodebough. Disability, 1862.

Lewis M. Thomas. Sergeant. Disability, February 3, 1863.

A. P. Stanley. Corporal. Disability, January 19, 1863.

John V. Vanderslice. Disability, April 20, 1863.

John Dales. Disability, 1862.

Thomas Swift. Disability.

John L. Dougherty. For wounds, December 8, 1863.

TRANSFERRED.

Henry Z. Lair. To Brigade band, December 31, 1862.

DESERTERS.

George Hampton. May 25, 1862.

Evan J. Paxon. And retaken.

Samuel Staiger. October, 1862.

ORGANIZATION OF C COMPANY, FIRST REGIMENT PENNSYLVANIA RESERVE CAVALRY.

Company C was recruited by Captain John P. Taylor and Lieutenant Wm. Mann, in Mifflin county, and organized on the 16th day of April, 1861, and offered its services to the State on the 17th, and was accepted on the 18th of the same month.

It was ordered to Harrisburg on the 20th day of April, 1861, and proceeded on the way, as far as Lewistown, when the order was countermanded. It was again ordered to report at Harrisburg on the 6th day of August, and arrived there on the 7th. Here Lieutenant John P. Taylor was elected captain, William Mann, Jr., first lieutenant, and William T. McEwen, second lieutenant, the company numbering eighty-two (82) men. It was mustered into the State service on the 10th day of August, 1861, by Colonel Taggart, and joined the regiment.

Arrived at Washington, D. C., on the 18th day of August, and mustered into the United Satets service on the 27th.

ENLISTED MEN OF C COMPANY.

Thomas A. Kearns, orderly sergeant.
J. Harvey Carson, first duty sergeant.
Michael Menges, second duty sergeant. Vet. vol., January 1, 1864. Wounded May 28, 1864.
Hamilton R. Mitchell, third duty sergeant.
Wilson P. Daughenbaugh, fourth duty sergeant.
George Way, fifth duty sergeant. Vet. vol., January 1, 1864. Wounded July 28, 1864.

Jacob Ruble, quarter-master sergeant.

Wilson S. Dellett, commissary-sergeant. Prisoner at Brandy Station, June 9, 1863.

John A. Davidsizer, first corporal. Vet. vol., January 1, 1864. Wounded May 9, 1864.

John Hoffman, second corporal. Vet. vol., January 1, 1864. Wounded July 28, 1864.

Charles A. Rice, third corporal.

William Ready, fourth corporal. Wounded July 28, 1864.

George White, fifth corporal. Vet. vol., January 1, 1864. Wounded May 9, 1864.

William Baird, sixth corporal.

John McMahon, seventh corporal. Vet. vol., January 1, 1864. Wounded June 21, 1864.

Anthony Assadalia, eighth corporal. Wounded at Fredericksburg December 12, 1862, also wounded May 28, 1864.

Graham, Geo. W. Wounded June 21, 1864.

Ackley, Joseph.

Brillhart, Robert M.

Betts, Robert

Cutler, Wm. D.

Cherry, John. Vet. vol., January 1, 1864.

Chirpman, James H.

Dippary, John.

Gates, J. K. Vet. vol., February 1, 1864.

Hooffnagle, H. N.

Jennings, Samuel N.

Latchford, Geo. W. Vet. vol., February 1, 1864.

Livingston, Joseph H., corporal. Wounded May 28, 1864.

Murray, James A. Vet. vol., February 1, 1864.
John McCann.
Nail, Henry H. Vet. vol., January 1, 1864. Wounded May 28, 1864.
Neitz, Percival. Prisoner at Brandy Station January 9, 1863. Wounded May 15, 1864.
Row, Charles.
Ruble, John. Vet. vol., February 1, 1864. Wounded July 28, 1864.
Stewart, Parmer
Scott, David C.
Slocum, Samuel. Vet. vol., Feb'y 1, 1864. Wounded June 21, 1864.
Seachrist, Christian
Sutton, John F.
Wable, John
Wilson, George W.
Wagner, Porter
Wiles, David
Yontz, William, prisoner August, 1864.
Luich, Lawrence
Clair, William. Wounded June 21, 1864.
Stillinger, William
Gifford, Geo. W.
Chamberlain, John
Derr, Jacob F.
Whitmore, Thomas. Wounded June 2, 1864.
Miller, G. W. Wounded June 21, 1864.
Kline, G. W. Wounded June 21, 1864.

PROMOTED.

Geo. W. Seachrist. To sergeant-major, October, 1861.

Robt. J. McNitt. Sergeant to second lieutenant, February 6, 1862.

John W. Nelson. Sergeant to second lieutenant, October 7, 1862.

James P. Landis, Sergeant to chief bugler, May 1, 1863.

Hiram McClenahen. Sergeant to first lieutenant, February 13, 1863.

KILLED.

Christian Romich, sergeant. Brandy Station June 9, 1863.

John H. Deal. Culpepper September 13, 1863

William Snyder, Cedar Mountain, August 9, 1863.

DIED.

Albert Laird, sergeant. Wounds received at Cedar Mountain, September 5, 1862.

Albert Strong, corporal. Typhoid fever, December 16, 1861.

John H. Yeager. Disease at Alexandria, June 26, 1863.

David A. Baker. May 16, 1862, from wound by accidental gun shot.

Jonathan Kring. Disease and wounds, in Alexandria, September, 1862.

William Lint. Disease, in Alexandria, August 21, 1862.

Abner N. McDonald, corporal. August 14, 1862, from wounds received at Cedar Mountain, August 9, 1862.

Amos Shank. October 24, of wound received at Auburn October 14, 1863.

Walker Scott, corporal. July 2, 1863, in Libby Prison, Richmond, of wounds received at Brandy Station June 9, 1863.

Marshall J. Stall. Disease, February 17, 1862.

DISCHARGED.

W. J. Furst, sergeant. Disability, September 1, 1862.

James B. Postlewaight. Disability.

James L. McDonald. Disability, June, 1862.

A. B. Selheimer. Disability, June, 1862.

William Barefoot. Disability, October, 1862.

Jesse Alexander. Disability, (wounds,) January, 1863.

Michael Bottorf, corporal. Disability, December 10, 1862.

Jacob Bottorf. Disability, March 9, 1863.

Martin Bottorf. Disability, September 9, 1862.

William Bradford. Disability.

Joseph M. Deveny. Disability.

William Kirlin. Disability, July 4, 1862.

Edwin Lochey, corporal. Disability, July 4, 1863.

Oliver H. McCalister. Disability, January 31, 1863.

James H. McClenahen. Disability, August 16, 1861.

James Robison. Disability, January 4, 1863.

Henry Swarm. Disability, May 23, 1862.

B. F. Stokes. Disability, November 8, 1861.

Edwin F. Teets. Disability, September 23, 1861.

Benj. Pollard. Disability, January 15, 1862.

W. V. B. Coplin. Corporal. Disability, January 19, 1863.

Samuel Ross. Disability, December 16, 1863.

TRANSFERRED.

John T. Murray. To Invalid Corps, August 18, 1863.

DESERTED.

John H. Ebbs. At Manassas, Va., June 28, 1862.
Felix Nolan. At Manassas, Va., June 28, 1862.
Paris Rolland. At Catletts, Va., April 28, 1862.

ORGANIZATION OF D COMPANY, FIRST REGIMENT PENNSYLVANIA RESERVE CAVALRY.

Company D was principally recruited at Lock Haven, Clinton county, Pennsylvania, from the counties of Cameron and Clinton, during the month of July, 1861.

The company was organized August the 17th, 1861, by the election of John W. Smith as captain, S. D. Barrow as first lieutenant, and Hugh A. McDonald as second lieutenant.

Was mustered into the State service, at Camp Curtin, Harrisburg, August the 21st, 1861, and was assigned to the First Regiment Pennsylvania Reserve Cavalry.

Left Harrisburg for Washington, August 23d, and mustered into the United States service August the 27th, 1861, at Camp Jones, Washington, D. C., where it joined the regiment.

ENLISTED MEN OF D COMPANY.

A. R. McDonald, orderly sergeant. Prisoner, August, 1862. Vet. vol., February, 1864.
Geo. M. Emery, first duty sergeant.

Thompson Snyder, second duty sergeant. Vet. vol., February 1, 1864. Wounded, June 21, 1864.

Charles H. Stetson, third duty sergeant. Wounded, May 28, 1864, and June 2, 1864.

Orlando H. Emery, fourth duty sergeant. Wounded, July 16, 1863, at Shepherdstown, Va.

Allen H. German, fifth duty sergeant. Vet. vol., February 1, 1864.

Geo. Misnonier, quartermaster sergeant. Vet. vol., February 1, 1864.

Thos J. Rockey, commissary sergeant.

Charles A. Moorse, first corporal. Vet. vol., February 1, 1864.

Horace Taylor, second corporal. Wounded at Cedar Mountain, August 9, 1862, and June 9, 1864. Vet. vol., February 1, 1864.

Henry Underham, third corporal. Vet. vol., February 1, 1864. Prisoner, June 21, 1864.

John C. Lewis, fourth corporal.

W. F. Lucore, fifth corporal. Wounded, June 21, 1864.

A. D. Rockey, sixth corporal. Vet. vol., February 1, 1864.

W. F. Moyer, seventh corporal. Vet. vol., February 1, 1864.

A. H. Lewis, eighth corporal Vet. vol., February 1, 1864. Wounded, June 21, 1864.

Tobias, H. R.

Aggy, H. R.

Coykendale, Philo

Carpenter, Levi S. Vet. vol., February 1, 1864.

Delany, William. Vet. vol., February 5, 1864. Wounded, June 28, 1864.

Delany, Henry. Vet. vol., February 1, 1864.

Davy, Eli C.

Frain, Jacob. Vet. vol., February, 1864.

Foster, Chester E. Vet. vol., February, 1864.

Grey, Isaiah. Vet. vol., February 1, 1864.

Herman Thomas. Vet. vol., Februrary 6, 1864. Killed, July 28, 1864.

Horton, William. Vet. vol., February 6, 1864. Prisoner, June 24, 1864.

Lewis, Alfred. Vet. vol., February 5, 1864.

Lord, Charles

Luid, Charles. Vet. vol., February 5, 1864.

Mitcheltree, Wm. H. Vet. vol., February 5, 1864. Wounded, July 28, 1864.

Miller, Wm.

Hendricks, Henry

Misner, Jacob B.

May, Charles. Vet. vol., February 5, 1864.

Miller, Benj. C.

Mahon, Warren. Prisoner, at Brandy Station, June 9, 1863.

Marony, John. Prisoner, June 24, 1864.

Marshall, George

Porchet, James. Vet. vol., February 1, 1864.

Pfoutz, Christopher. Bugler. Vet. vol., February 1, 1864.

Richardson, John D.

Ragan, Jeremiah

Sorrell, Nelson

Salada, Frederick. Vet. vol., February 1, 1864.

Stevenson B. Wounded May 28, 1864.

Thomas, Charles

Williams, Wm. T. Vet. vol., February 6, 1864.

Walizer, Jonathan. Vet. vol., February 6, 1864. Wounded, July 28, 1864.

Cridler, William. Vet. vol., February 6, 1864.

Lucore, Lemuel. Prisoner, at Cedar Mountain, August 9, 1862.

McKinney, Charles. Vet. vol., February 1, 1864 Prisoner, November, 1862.

Butcher, Frank. Prisoner, June 13, 1862.

Miller, John

Taylor, Henry C.

Roark, John

Sunderland, Samuel. Vet. vol., February, 1864.

PROMOTED.

Wm. F. Butcher. Sergeant to second lieutenant, July 5, 1862.

Marcus L. French. Sergeant to second lieutenant, 1861.

Warren L. Holbrook. Sergeant to second lieutenant, 1861.

Philip H. Walker. Sergeant to second lieutenant, September 9, 1862.

KILLED.

John A. Tibbins. At Brandy Station, Va., June 9, 1863.

R. P. Hughling. Corporal. At Cedar Mountain, Va., August 9, 1862.

Gregor McGregor. Sergeant. At Cedar Mountain, Va., August 9, 1862.

Joseph Hughling. In skirmish at Drainesville. November 27, 1861.

DIED.

James L. Barr. October 16, 1863, of wounds received at Auburn, Va., October 14, 1863.

Charles C. Daniels. August 16, of wounds received at Cedar Mountain, Va., August 9, 1862.

John L. Knight. Disease, October 31, 1861.

Wm. B. Rogers. Wounds, September 9, 1862.

W. P. Stewart. Disease, at Warrenton, Va., September 13, 1863.

Angus McDonald. Disease, November, 1862.

Rufus Roudenberg. Disease, November, 1862.

Ellis Perry. December 18, 1863, of wounds received November 27, 1863.

DISCHARGED.

Charles Amiden Disability, November 18, 1862.

B. M. P. Baird. Wounds, December 16, 1862.

Almarion Chapman. Disability, September 13, 1863. Twice taken prisoner.

Benjamin Emery. December 24, 1862.

Alexander H. Gabe. Disability, February 12, 1863.

Alexander Henderson. Corporal. Disability, March 26, 1863.

Wm. Johnson. Disability, December 10, 1862.

Daniel Kester. Disability, January 13, 1863.

A. D. Ligget. Disability, October 25, 1863.

John Luich. Disability, March 14, 1863.

Mortimer Longwell. Corporal. Disability, March 14, 1863.

James Misner. Wounds, January 26, 1863, received at Cedar Mountain, August 19, 1862.

Charles McIntyre. Disability, August 10, 1861.

John Passal. Disability, May 16, 1862.

Wm. A. Quiggle. Corporal. Wounds at Cedar Mountain, August 9, 1862.

J. R. Racard. Corporal. Disability, November 18, 1861.

Elias Rossman. Disability, April 28, 1863.

Calvin P. Russel. Disability, March 19, 1863.

B. F. Straw. December 24, 1862, from wounds received at Cedar Mountain, August 9, 1862.

David W. Tibbens. Disability, January 13, 1863.

John Whiteman. Disability, April 10, 1863.

John H. Ruir. Disability, May 11, 1862.

Charles Anderson. Disability, January 9, 1863.

TRANSFERRED.

R. J. Davison. To the First Regiment Pennsylvania Reserve Rifles, December 16, 1861.

DESERTED.

Abraham R Brant. Near Manassas, Va, June 18, 1862.

Samuel D. Fuller. Near Catalett, Va., April 29, 1862.

Henry S. Hoffman. Near Manassas, Va., June, 1862.

Wm. Jones. October, 1862.

Russel Miller. At time of enlistment, 1861.

John Rubert. At time of enlistment, 1861.

Joseph Hilsher. July, 1863.

ORGANIZATION OF E COMPANY, FIRST REGIMENT PENNSYLVANIA RESERVE CAVALRY.

Company E was principally recruited in Centre county, Pennsylvania, by Captain Jonathan Wolf, with some few recruits from Clinton and Clearfield counties.

Was organized on the 19th day of March, 1861, and left for Harrisburg on the 25th day of July, 1861, and arrived at Washington, D. C., August the 18th, where it was attached to the regiment.

ENLISTED MEN OF E COMPANY.

William C. Wilky, orderly sergeant. Wounded July 16, 1863.

Jesse Fry, first duty sergeant. Vet. vol., January 1, 1864.

John Craft, second duty sergeant. Vet. vol., February 20, 1864. Wounded, July 28, 1864.

H. H. McCullough, third duty sergeant. Killed June 24, 1864.

Edwin B. Holt, fourth duty sergeant. Vet. vol., February 20, 1864.

John Williams, fifth duty sergeant.

Walter S. Lint, quartermaster-sergeant. Vet. vol., February 1, 1864 Wounded June 21, 1864.

William Wilson, commissary-sergeant.

Wm. H. Buck, first corporal. Vet. vol., January 1, 1864. Prisoner at Cedar Mountain August 9, 1863.

Jacob Raymond, second corporal

Wm. Lowery, third corporal. Wounded at Brandy Station June 9, 1863. Killed May 28, 1864.

Samuel J. Krotzer, fourth corporal.

Wm. N. Esworthy, fifth corporal. Vet. vol., February 20, 1864. Mortally wounded June 21, 1864.

Alvy, Marion, bugler.

Checkman, Henry. Vet. vol., February 20, 1864.

Cheeseman, John

Dewitt, Martin. Wounded May 9, 1864.

Fulton, James. Vet. vol. January 1, 1864.

Grassmire, William

Garrett, William

Grant, Thomas W. Vet. vol., January 1, 1864. Prisoner July 28, 1864.

Gault, James V. Vet. vol., January 1, 1864. Wounded June 21, 1864.

Hunter, Daniel W. Wounded at New Hope Church, November 27, 1863.

Hatter, Joseph. Prisoner June 24, 1864. Vet. vol., January 1, 1864.

Kress, Mortimer

Keys, Stanley A. Vet. vol., January 1, 1864.

Keys, Charles

Kearns, Pat. B. Wounded August 14, 1864.

Laughman, Donas. Vet. vol., February. Prisoner at Brandy Station June 9, 1863.

McMullen, Frank A. Vet. vol., February 1, 1864.

Neiman, A. B. Prisoner November 16, 1863.

Null, John. Wounded at New Hope Church, November 27, 1863.

Parr, Joseph. Vet. vol., January 1, 1864.

Rodger, Alfred
Reese, Valentine. Wounded June 1, 1864.
Reider, James
Struble, John C. Vet. vol., January 1, 1864.
Saxton, Timothy. Vet. vol., February 1, 1864.
Switzer, Crawford
Smith, David
Shirk, William
Shaffer, William. Mortally wounded June 21, 1864.
Tate, David.
Wilson, William
Watson, Stanley
Wyland, William. Vet. vol., February 1, 1864.
Toomis, George. Wounded May 28, 1864.
Carney, Joseph
Vonlear. William
Gault, John
Yeager, John
Derr, Samuel

PROMOTED.

Johnston C. Akers. Sergeant to first lieutenant, June 16, 1863.
John A. Bayard. To first lieutenant, December, 1862.
Charles L. Buffington. To battalion adjutant, March, 1862.
Amos M. Herrick. Sergeant to second lieutenant, February 13, 1863.
Samuel Lipton. Sergeant to second lieutenant.
Jeremiah Newman. Sergeant to first lieutenant, March, 1862.

DIED.

George Bruss. Hospital, 1862.
John Cook, corporal. Disease, November 18, 1862.
Thomas B. Fenton. Disease, March 18, 1862.
Charles R. Fells, corporal. Disease, August, 1863.
Witherite William. Disease, October, 1863.

DISCHARGED.

Thomas R. Anderson. Disability.
Henry Atkins, sergeant. Disability.
John C. Bradley. Disability, January 15, 1863.
William T. Buck. Disability, December, 1862.
Henry J. Boell. Disability, March, 1863.
John H. Fox. Disability, August, 1861.
Michael Fausey. Disability, February 18, 1863.
Peter Gesiwite. Disability, August 27, 1861.
Rankin Hollabaugh. Disability, February, 1862.
Frank Heckendorn. Disability, September, 1862.
James M. Howe, sergeant. Disability, January 13, 1863.
George James. Disability, February, 1862.
James Keys. Disability, February, 1862.
Levi Kline. Disability, November, 1861.
Des Cartes Kelly. Disability, March, 1863.
Henry Klapp. Disability, January, 1862.
William C. Murray, sergeant. Disability, February, 1862.
Eli Mercer. Disability, April, 1862.
James Miller. Disability, December, 1862.
Samuel Mills. Disability, February, 1862.
Bernard Morrison. Disability, January, 1862.

Abraham Miller. Disability, December, 1863.
Hugh Martin. Dishonorably discharged for disability, January 7, 1864.
Milton Neiman. Disability, November, 1862.
John Osborn. Disability, April, 1862.
Fenton Phalon. Disability, February, 1863.
Reuben Roup. Disability, March, 1863.
William Summers. Disability, November, 1861.
Joseph Shoup. Disability, September, 1862.
Rufus Stratton. Disability, September 16, 1862.
Henry D. Sands. Disability, October 9, 1862.
John H. Thomas. Disability, August, 1862.
Joseph Schlem, corporal. Disability, February 6, 1863.
David R. Wiser. Disability, January, 1862.
Calvin Wolf. Disability, April 6, 1863.
John W. Ward. Disability, March, 1863.
Philip Wenterodd. Disability, October, 1862.

TRANSFERRED.

Thompson Wilson, Invalid Corps.

DESERTED.

Arthur Swisher. March 7, 1863.

ORGANIZATION OF F COMPANY, FIRST REGIMENT PENNSYLVANIA RESERVE CAVALRY.

Company F was enlisted by Captain J. M Harper, about the latter part of July and beginning of August, 1861, at Carmichael's, Green county, Pennsylvania.

Started for Camp Curtin, at Harrisburg, on the

15th day of August, was organized on the 17th, and sworn into the United States service on the 24th, by Captain Hastings, and attached to the regiment.

Leaving Camp Curtin, the company arrived at Camp Jones, on the 27th day of August, 1861.

ENLISTED MEN OF F COMPANY.

Jonas E. Lucas, orderly sergeant. Prisoner by guerrillas, November 17, 1863.

John H. Black, first duty sergeant.

James K. Gregg, second duty sergeant. Wounded at Auburn, Va., October 14, 1863.

Geo. W. Evans, third duty sergeant.

John Haver, fourth duty sergeat.

John R. Dunlap, fifth duty sergeant. Wounded on picket, November, 1863.

Vincent Worthington, quartermaster sergeant. Vet. vol., February 1, 1864.

J. H. Hoge, commissary sergeant. Wounded at Brandy Station, June 9, 1863.

Wm. H. H. Eberhart, first corporal. Vet. vol., February 23, 1864.

M. V. B. Mercer, second corporal.

John Jones, third corporal.

Samuel W. Dugan, fourth corporal.

Alvin H. Wilson, fifth corporal.

Joseph H. Shaffer, sixth corporal. Vet. vol., February 1, 1864. Prisoner, June 24, 1864.

Jesse Hughes, seventh corporal. Vet. vol., February 13, 1864. Wounded August 22, 1864.

Thomas F. Reppert, eighth corporal. Wounded July 28, 1864.

Seaton, Geo. W.
Worthington, James, bugler.
Rhinehart, David H., bugler.
Harne, William. Vet. vol., February 1, 1864.
Anderson, John. Vet. vol., February 1, 1864.
Alfred, Asa S. Wounded, May 5, 1864.
Alexander, Morris
Baker, David S. Vet. vol., February 1, 1864.
Brestel Omet.
Brown, James W. Prisoner, August, 1862, and November 17, 1863.
Cummings, James R. Vet. vol., February 13, 1864.
Crayne, Isaac B.
Cree, Joseph M.
Cox, James
Davis, Winchester
Dean, John W.
Fisher, Franklin
Craigo, Thomas. Prisoner, June 24, 1864.
Hight, Peter A.
Hughes, James
Houseman, Sam'l S. Vet. vol., February 3, 1864.
Jones, Oliver
McFarland, John F.
Mayhorn, Nelson. Vet. vol., February 1, 1864.
Midlam, Enoch W. Prisoner, at Brandy Station, January 9, 1863.
Neff, John
Neff, Abraham. Vet. vol., February 1, 1864.
Phillips, James W. Prisoner, on picket, November 17, 1863.
Ross, Samuel

Shape, Demos J. Wounded and prisoner at Brandy Station, June 9, 1863.
Shawmon, John F.
Walters, John W. Wounded, May 9, 1864.
Walters, John A.
Young, Andrew J. Vet. vol., February 13, 1864.
Long, Nelson
Evans, Robert
Fordyce, Justus G. Wounded July 28, 1864.
Ross, Ira. Prisoner at Brandy Station, June 9, 1863. Wounded, June 21, 1864.
Crawford, George W.
Hummel, David
Hill, Samuel
Grove, James P.
Johnston, George W. L.
Brestel, Jacob. Wounded, May 28, 1864.
Grimm, David C.
Maple, David
Carry, Sylvester P.
Eisiminger, James
Mitchell, Jacob
Zollars, Richard S.
Ely, Caleb. Wounded at Auburn, Va., October 14, 1863.
Crawford, G. W. Prisoner, June 24, 1864.
Ruble, James. Wounded at Brandy Station, June 9, 1863.
Illguifritz, D. F.
Toomey, Isaiah
Grassmire, Albert
Herene, Edward

Gresley, Charles. Prisoner at New Hope Church, November 27, 1863.

Poleman, Wm. K. Prisoner at New Hope Church, November 27, 1863.

Grass, Henry. Prisoner on the Rapidann river, September 15, 1863.

Kridel, Frederick W.

Phillips, Addison. Wounded May 10, 1864.

Mairs, Samuel

Cree, H. C. Wounded at Auburn, Va., October 14, 1863.

Phillips, J. A.

Lightner, Josiah

Shawmon, J. W.

Craigo, James. Mortally wounded, May 28, 1864.

Harne, A. M. Wounded, June 21, 1864.

PROMOTED.

Levi K. Evans. Sergeant to second lieutenant, November 14, 1861.

Sam'l S. Greenlee. Sergeant to second lieutenant, June 13, 1862.

H. A. Wood. To Reg't C. S., June 16, 1862.

Thomas Lucas. To second lieutenant, June, 1862.

KILLED.

George W. Teagarden. Killed at Mount Jackson, Va., June 3, 1862.

Abner Murdock. Killed, July 12, 1864.

DIED.

Geo. W. Beam. Disease, December 16, 1863.

Samuel R. Dunlap. Disease, January 13, 1863.
William Evans. Disease, January 19, 1862.
William Jones. Disease, July 16, 1862.
Samuel Houlsworth. Sergeant. Disease, November 27, 1861.
David L. Keener. Disease, July 12, 1863.
Anthony Fraunk. Disease, December 29, 1863.

DISCHARGED.

James Alton. Disability, September 22, 1862.
Thomas Berch. Disability, March 11, 1863
James P. Crawford. Disability, October 17, 1862.
Wm. Cummings. Disability, January 4, 1862
Hugh D. Cree. Disabled, January 4,1862.
Harrison Gump. Disability, April 20, 1863.
John W. Hopkins. Disability, December 4, 1862.
Henry S. Jenkins. Disability, January 19, 1862.
James R. Kendel. Disability, January 28, 1862.
Wm. McClelland. Disability, January 28, 1863.
Geo. W. McClelland. Disability, February 16, 1863.
John F. McCullough. By order, January 16, 1862.
Thomas H. Nutt. Disability, December 16, 1862.
William Rush. Disability, January 27, 1863.
John M. Shape. Disability, April 29, 1863.
Richard D. Simners. Disability, June 7, 1862.
Philip L. Kramer. Disability, January 4, 1862.
B. K. Higgenbotham. Disability, March 6, 1862.
Lawrence B. Craft. Disability, July 28, 1862.
Simeon S. Lucas. Disability, September, 18, 1863.
Smith Steaton. Disability, December 8, 1862.
James H. Fordyce. Disability, March 13, 1863.
Newton Kigly. By order, May 26, 1863.

TRANSFERRED.

Henry B. King. To Invalid Corps, 1863.

DESERTERS.

None.

ORGANIZATION OF G COMPANY, FIRST REGIMENT PENNSYLVANIA RESERVE CAVALRY.

The formation of Company G was commenced by Captain Jacob Higgins, at Hollidaysburg, Blair county, Pennsylvania, from a volunteer company called the Blair County Dragoons.

About the middle of August, 1861, having collected a few men as a nucleus, he proceeded with them to Camp Curtin, Harrisburg, where with part of a company from Lisburn, Cumberland county, and recruits collected while in camp, the company was filled and its organization completed, by the election of Jacob Higgins, captain, David Gardner, first lieutenant, and H. S. Thomas, second lieutenant.

This company having been principally recruited at Harrisburg, during the return of the three months men, was collected from all parts of the State, and among its members has representatives from thirty-two different counties.

The company was mustered into the State service, August the 22d, and into the United States service, August the 28th, 1861, when it was assigned to the First Pennsylvania Reserve Cavalry.

It arrived in Washington, August the 29th, where it joined the regiment.

ENLISTED MEN OF G COMPANY.

Samuel Kilpatrick, orderly sergeant. Vet. vol., February 1, 1864.

John O. Clark, first duty sergeant. Vet. vol., March 10, 1864.

Geo. W. Cyphers, second duty sergeant.

Francis S. Spiegel, third duty sergeant. Vet. vol., January 1, 1864.

John W. Bruner, fourth duty sergeant. Taken prisoner June 9, 1863. Vet. vol., January 1, 1864. Transferred to Signal Corps.

R. G. Howerter, fifth duty sergeant.

John Rohrbaugh, commissary sergeant. Vet. vol, February 1, 1864.

Thomas McGinly, quartermaster sergeant. Vet. vol., January 1, 1864.

John W. Taylor, first corporal. Prisoner, June 24, 1864.

John D. Richards, second corporal. Wounded, June 24, 1864.

Philip Seiferts, third corporal.

H. C. Portner, fourth corporal. Vet. vol., January 1, 1864. Mortally wounded June 21, 1864.

Jerome Kishbaugh, fifth corporal. Prisoner, June 9, 1863. Wounded, May 28, 1864.

Isaac Kennedy, sixth corporal. Regimental color-bearer.

Samuel Reese, seventh corporal.

Fritz, Wm. D., Vet. vol., January 1, 1864.

McDonald, James M. Died in hospital.

Corl, Abram. Wounded at battle of Bull Run, August 30, 1862, also July 28, 1864.

Greaves, Francis S.
Adams, George
Buch, Milton, bugler.
Campbell, Daniel
Cory, Warren R. Wounded at Culpepper, Va., September 13, 1863.
Campbell, William. Vet. vol., January 1, 1864. Transferred to Signal Corps.
Delancy, Wm. P.
Downs, Adam
Ells, Wm.
Farnwalt, Isaac
Grey, Mercer. Wounded, June 21, 1864.
Hawn, Samuel K. Mortally wounded at St. Mary's Church, June 24, 1864.
Highler, Adam. Vet. vol., January 1, 1864.
Griffin, John
Hisner, Michael
Hull, Robert. P. Prisoner at Sulphur Springs, Va., August, 1862.
Hughey, Samuel
Kritzer, James
Lantz, John, bugler. Vet. vol., January 1, 1864.
McFarland, Daniel. Vet. vol., January 1, 1864; and a prisoner August 1, 1862.
Mullin, Patrick. Vet. vol., January 1, 1864.
Munch, Wm. Drowned, May 17, 1864, in James river.
Newman, David W.
Page H. W. Vet. vol., January 1, 1864. Killed May 21, 1864.
Reed, John M.
Reese, William. Vet. vol., January 1, 1864.

Rhoads, William, blacksmith.
Rhoads, Adam
Snell, Aaron. Vet. vol., January 1, 1864, and wounded at New Hope Church, November 27, 1863.
Shawley, Henry, blacksmith.
Stoner, Leonard
Wike, William, teamster.
Ely, William, saddler.
Hall, Wilmer C.
Failes, Horace
Bently, Abram. Wounded at Brandy Station, Va., June 9, 1863.
Platt, Hiram. Promoted to first sergeant.
Pugh, Evan. Wounded at Brandy Station, June 9, 1863.
Gilliland, Samuel
Higby, Charles
Cory, George A.
Stewart, Charles R.
Wiggins, Daniel. Wounded, August, 1862.
Hartsock, Thomas
Hatch, Arthur
James Benninghoff. Severely wounded and prisoner at New Hope Church, Va., November 27, 1863.

PROMOTED.

H. C. Beamer. Sergeant-major to first lieutenant, May, 1862.
F. P. Confer. Sergeant to second lieutenant, September, 1862.
Alonzo Reed. Sergeant to second lieutenant, November 24, 1862.

George J. Geiser. Sergeant-major to second lieutenant, April 12, 1863.

Wm. P. Lloyd. Private to hospital steward, December 18, 1862.

John McCahan. Private to commissary sergeant, January 28, 1863.

DIED.

William Grey. December 27, 1862.

Cyrus Rosenberger. January 7, 1863.

DISCHARGED.

William Hoffman. Disability, 1862.

George W. Briggs, corporal. Disability, March, 1862.

John S. Stubbs, corporal. Disability, October 1, 1861.

Jacob Boyer. Disability, January, 1863.

William Boyer. Disability, February 1862.

George Fulleton. Disability, March 18, 1863, from wounds.

George W. Fisher. Disability, September, 1862.

David H. Gates. Disability, August, 1862, from wounds.

Joseph Gonder. Disability, March, 1862.

Jonathan Harper. Disability, March, 1862.

John Lewis. Disability, September, 1861, from wounds.

James McCahan. Disability, February, 1862.

Samuel D. Palsgrove. Disability, April, 1863.

Daniel Rittle. Disability, April, 1863, from wound.

Albert Ruggles. Disability, 1862.

Horatio Rembaugh. Disability, February, 1863.

Joseph Rocks. Disability, 1862.

Peter W. Swoap. Disability, October, 1862.
John Seabolt, Disability, March, 1862.
Zac. Welty. Disability, January 18, 1868.
John Uhler. Accidental wound, August, 1862.
Chas. H. Hutchison. Disability, January, 1863.
Wm. Strickland, sergeant. Disability, March, 1862.

TRANSFERRED.

James M. Adams, corporal. To second lieutenant Corps de Afrique.
Russel Bailets. Invalid Corps, September, 1863.
John C. McCullough. Invalid Corps, September, 1863.
Ernest Conzler. Regular army, November, 1862.

DESERTERS.

Hiram Crowl. Time of enlistment.
Julius Eicholtz. Time of enlistment
Lawrence Fought. Time of enlistment.
James Fulleton. Time of enlistment
Jonathan Kilmore. Time of enlistment.
John C. Kristy Time of enlistment.
Israel Meyers. December 1, 1861.
John A. Orner. Time of enlistment.
John Williams. April 11, 1863.

ORGANIZATION OF H COMPANY, FIRST REGIMENT PENNSYLVANIA RESERVE CAVALRY.

Company H was organized in Fayette county, Pennsylvania, by Captain James B. Davidson, some two or three years previous to the commencement of the rebellion, and was known as the "Dunlap Creek Cavalry."

Shortly after the First Bull Run battle, the company tendered its services to the United States, and was accepted. On the first day of August, 1861, it left for Camp Wilkins, at Pittsburg, and on the fourth day of August was sworn into the United States service.

On the twenty-seventh day of August, the company left Camp Wilkins for Washington, D. C., where it arrived on the twenty-ninth; and on the sixth day of September was mustered into the United States service, and joined to the regiment.

ENLISTED MEN OF H COMPANY.

Joseph Hostetler, orderly sergeant. Vet. vol., February 16, 1863. Wounded, May 9, 1864.

George B. Kingsland, first duty sergeant. Prisoner at New Hope Church, November 27, 1863.

Benjamin F. Hibbs, second duty sergeant. Wounded, May 28, 1864.

William Phillips, third duty sergeant.

Harrison Mann, fourth duty sergeant.

Cyrus A. Porter, quarter-master sergeant.

James Normine, commissary sergeant.

James O. Llewellen, first corporal

George Brown, second corporal. Wounded May 9, 1864, and August 14, 1864.

Robert F. Hibbs, third corporal.

John M. Watson, fourth corporal. Vet. vol., February 16, 1864.

Henry Keifer, fifth corporal. Vet. vol., Feb. 16, 1864.

Isaac Richey, sixth corporal. Vet. vol., Feb. 16, 1864.

Robert Thompson, seventh corporal. Wounded, May 28, 1864.

William Glunt, eighth corporal.

James P. Scott, bugler.

Edward Hunt, blacksmith.

Isaac Brewer, farrier.

David Matthers, saddler.

Smith, Jeremiah

McMullin, Albert. Prisoner, at Culpepper, September 13, 1863.

Warner, Thomas E.

Houseman, Thomas

Vanhorn, James D. Prisoner, October 22, 1863. Killed, July 28, 1864.

Nutt, Joseph E. Prisoner, June 21, 1864.

Potter, Henry

Arnold Albert H. Prisoner, June 21, 1864.

Adams, John. Vet. vol., February 16, 1864.

Algeo, Charles. Wounded at Auburn Mills, October 14, 1863.

Algeo, David. Wounded June 21, 1864.

Byers, David A.

Cox, John F. Wounded, May 7, 1864.

Cox, Robert B.

Davidson, Jeremiah

Dickenson, William. Wounded, May 28, 1864.

Davis, Isaiah

Dickenson, John P. Wounded, May 9, 1864.

Fall, John B.

Gregg, Elmer

Gaskill, William

Garrett, Joseph. Prisoner, December 15, 1863, by guerrillas.
Grooms, Thomas
Gue, Robert
Hively, James
Handlin James
Jenkins, Thomas. Wounded, May 28, 1864.
Logan, Jackson. Vet. vol., February 1, 1864.
McCaen, Lewis
Michaels, Wm. H.
Marshall, John F. Vet. vol., February 1, 1864.
McFall, Samuel. Vet. vol., February 16, 1864.
Minehart, William W.
Maloney, Peter
Normine, Thomas. Prisoner at Culpepper, September 13, 1863.
Rictor, John E.
Reid, Wm. F. Prisoner, October 25, 1863.
Richey, Wm. A. Prisoner, October 25, 1863.
Shields, Wm.
Vankirk, John. Wounded, May 28, 1864.
Walker, Barnabas W. Vet. vol., February 1, 1864.
Work, George T.
Wilson, Marrion
Leech, James
McCaffrey, James. Wounded, June 2, 1864.
Everhart, Wentel
Calligan, George
Nicholson, Thomas. Prisoner, September 6, 1863.
Wilson, Jasper
Normine, John S.
Wimer, James

Galaher, Daniel
Denny, John A.
Edmonds, Wm.
Johnston, Thomas A. Killed at Gettysburg, July 2, 1863.

PROMOTED.

Wm. S. Craft. Orderly sergeant to first lieutenant, October 22, 1862.
John D. Scott, Private to first lieutenant, November 21, 1861.
Eli S. Forsyth. Sergeant to second lieutenant, February 12, 1863.
James Jackson. Sergeant to second lieutenant, September, 1861.

DIED.

Madison Davies. Disease, at Alexandria, Va., December, 1862.
Moses B. Ewing. Disease, at Washington, September, 1862,
William Stewart. Disease, at Camp Pierpont, Va., December 17, 1861.

DISCHARGED.

James P. Walker. Disability, February 17, 1863.
Wm. W. Messmore. Disability, March 27, 1862.
Daniel Fearer. Disability, February 5, 1863.
John C. Bird. Disability, February 4, 1863.
Charles P. Coats. Disability, December 31, 1861.
John W. Chalfant. Disability, December 31, 1861.
James Fawcit. Disability, 1862.

Alexander Johns. Disability, April 12, 1862.
John Litton. Disability, October 7, 1863.
Alexander Lane. Disability, 1862.
Wm. W Melchi. Disability, January 13, 1863.
Vincent Owens. Disability, December 31, 1861.
John A. Rice. Disability.
Wm. Sewenger. Disability, January 13, 1863.
Henry Tate. Disability, April 8, 1862.
James Varner. Disability, December 31, 1861.
James McCune. Disability, 1862.

TRANSFERRED.

Edson Sturgeon. To Sixth U. S. Cavalry, October, 1861.
Wm. A. Vanhorn. To Invalid Corps, 1863.

DESERTED.

Jesse S. P. Balsinger. From Hospital, 1862.
Wm. Bennett. At Aquia creek, Va., 1863.
James C. Greene. At Alexandria, Va., 1862.
Wm. M. Remmel. From Hospital, April, 1862.
Rob't W. Shroyer. At Mt Jackson, Va., June 30, 1862.
Alexander Price. July, 1863.

ORGANIZATION OF I COMPANY, FIRST REGIMENT PENNSYLVANIA RESERVE CAVALRY.

Company I, First Regiment Pennsylvania Reserve Cavalry, made up of citizens of different parts of Washington county, Pennsylvania, is a part of what was once the "Winfield Hussars," an old volunteer organization, commanded by then Major W. W. McNulty.

This company was sworn into the State service by Captain Robert Patterson, at Pittsburg, Pennsylvania, on the 13th, day of August, 1861. Left Pittsburg August the 26th, for Washington, D. C., in company with several other organizations, comprising what was then know as the Sixth Regiment Pennsylvania Cavalry, and went into camp on Seventh street.

On the 6th day of September, 1861, the company was mustered into the United States service.

The regiment to which it was then attached, failing to complete its organization, was disbanded by order of General McClellan, and this company, together with two other companies, was incorporated with the First Regiment Pennsylvania Reserve Cavalry, of which it is now a part.

ENLISTED MEN OF I COMPANY.

Samuel T. Work, orderly sergeant. Wounded, August 14, 1864.

James D. Scott, first duty sergeant.

Alex'r C. Elliott, second duty sergeant. Vet. vol., January 1, 1864. Wounded, June 21, 1864.

John L. Mustard, third duty sergeant. Wounded, June 21, 1864.

Rob't D. Wilkin, fourth duty sergeant.

David Pollock, fifth duty sergeant.

Samuel W. McKee, quartermaster sergeant. Wounded June 21, 1864.

Patrick H. McNulty, commissary sergeant. Wounded, May 28, 1864.

Hillary Wilson, first corporal.

Thomas Richmond, second corporal.

David McGuigan, third corporal. Wounded, May 28, 1864.

Lewis Kramer, fourth corporal, color guard.

Beacroft, George

Berwick, Franklin. Vet. vol., January 1, 1864.

Bitts, Samuel T. Taken prisoner twice.

Crider, William

Clyde, John

Curtis, Wm. A. Vet. vol., January 1, 1864.

Conau, Thomas H.

Essick, Rudolph

Gibson, John. Vet. vol., January 1, 1864.

Gaumer, Moses

Garrett, Samuel

Groff, John

Johnson, Walter

Loughead, John. Vet. vol., January 1, 1864.

McConkey, Isaac. Vet. vol., January 1, 1864.

McConkey, Smithson. Vet. vol., January 1, 1864, killed.

McKinley, John. Prisoner by guerrillas, September 6, 1863.

McCormick, Walter S.

McCarroll, Wm.

Murray, Chester, bugler.

McCall, William

Newell, Archibald

Patterson, Thomas. Prisoner by guerrillas, September 6, 1863. Died March 30, 1864, at Hospital Annapolis, Md.

Patten, Wm. P.

Robertson, John L. Vet. vol., January 1, 1864.
Rosenberger, Alexander. Prisoner.
Richmond, David
Rippey, Wm. J.
Smiley, James
Sauppe, John G.
Wells, Grafton. Vet. vol., January 1, 1864.
McElroy, William
La Barr, George J. Vet. vol., February 1, 1864.
Bingham, John A. Wounded, May 9, 1864.
Morrow, Charles. Vet. vol., February 1, 1864.
Milligan, Peter. Prisoner by guerrillas, September 6, 1863.

PROMOTED.

James M. Gaston. Sergeant to second lieutenant, August 24, 1861.
George W. Lyon. Sergeant to second lieutenant, February 12, 1863.
T. C. McGregor. Sergeant to second lieutenant, May 10, 1862.
Francis S. Morgan. Sergeant to first lieutenant, February 12, 1863.
T. R. Storer. Chief bugler, October, 1861.
Jacob Wolf. Regimental veterinary surgeon, April, 1863.
J. B. Richey. Sergeant to second lieutenant.

KILLED.

David Ackelson, corporal. Near King George Court House, April 26, 1863.
James Barry, corporal. By guerrillas, September 6, 1863.

Eli Leskelett. Near King George Court House, Va., April 26, 1863.

Moses Hastings, corporal. Near King George Court House, Va., April 26, 1863.

Thomas Richmond, corporal. May 21, 1864, Milford Station, Va.

Smithson McConkey. May 21, 1864, Milford Station, Va.

DIED.

George W. Gist. Disease, December, 1861.

Jacob George. Disease, December, 1861.

James W. McKee. Accidental gun-shot, January, 1862.

Thomas Parkes. Disease, January 18, 1862.

Wm. M. Porter. Disease, September 28, 1862.

John G. Wells, sergeant. Disease, February 26, 1862.

DISCHARGED.

Alexander Berwick. Disability, April 15, 1862.

John Beacroft. Disability, December 24, 1861.

Andrew Crouch. Disability, April 15, 1862.

Thomas Dunkel. Disability, January 1, 1862.

John F. Foust. Disability, April 15, 1862.

John H. Gaston, corporal. Disability, October 27, 1862.

Joshua J. Hunter. Disability, April 15, 1862.

James Miller, Jr. Disability, December 23, 1862.

James Miller, Sen. Disability, December 23, 1862.

Andrew F. McClure. Disability, January 15, 1863.

Wm. F. Patten. Disability, February 13, 1863.

Louis Quilland. Disability, January 15, 1863.

John Richmond, sergeant. Disability, October 6, 1862.
Wm. H. Rose. Disability, June, 1862.
Wm. F. Smith. Disability, March 1, 1862.
Alexander L. Williams. Disability, August 16, 1862.
Alexander R. Wythe, sergeant. Disability, December, 1861.
Wm. Denniston, sergeant. Disability, April 2, 1863.
Lorenzo A. Rice. Disability, June 2, 1862.
William C. Richey, corporal. Disability, October, 1862.

TRANSFERRED.

None.

DESERTED.

Edward Powelson. January 17, 1862.
Thomas G. Dowling, June 17, 1862.

ORGANIZATION OF K COMPANY, FIRST REGIMENT PENNSYLVANIA RESERVE CAVALRY.

Company K is composed of men from Allegheny and Washington counties.

Before entering the service, they formed two volunteer organizations, known as the "National Lancers," of Allegheny county, commanded by Captain W. Boyce; and the "Union Cavalry," of Finleyville, Washington county, commanded by Captain A. Borland.

About one week before entering the service, the two companies joined, and formed one organization, called the "National Cavalry," commanded by Captain W. Boyce.

A portion of the company enlisted August the 28th,

1861, and the rest September the 3d, 1861, at Pittsburg, Pennsylvania.

Was sworn in on the 3d of September, by Colonel A. Hays.

Left Pittsburg on the 4th, and arrived in Washington, D. C., on September the 7th.

When it arrived in Washington, it was assigned to the Sixth regiment Pennsylvania Cavalry. Mustered into service on the 6th day of September.

The Sixth regiment being disbanded, the company was assigned to the First Regiment Pennsylvania Reserve Cavalry, on the 27th day of September, of which it is now a part.

ENLISTED MEN OF K COMPANY.

A. B. Darrah, orderly sergeant.
J. A. Latimer, first duty sergeant.
J. W. Boyce, second duty sergeant.
Rob't Boyce, quartermaster sergeant.
J. Patterson, commissary sergeant
J. M. Boyce, first corporal. Prisoner, June 21, 1864.
S. F. Ralston, second corporal.
J. Connelly, third corporal.
T. Westerman, fourth corporal.
S. R. Patten, fifth corporal.
McClure, Wm. J.
Kiefer, John, bugler. Prisoner, at Sulphur Springs, August 22, 1862.
McCombs, Thomas
Trumble, John
Feather, Joseph
Anderson, John

Boyce, Thomas D.
Coup, George
Curran, Edward
Calohan, Charles A.
Cox, Abraham
Dilks, Charles P. Prisoner, November 17, 1863, by guerrillas.
Duncan, John M.
Flanegan, Hugh
Gordon, William
Herriott, John
Herrell, Wilson
Hanna, Jacob
Jones, Thomas. Vet. vol., February 1, 1864. Prisoner, June 21, 1864.
Keifer, Samuel
Kennedy, Joseph M.
Lessnutt, Richard
Maradith, John. Prisoner, at Bealton Station, October 14, 1863.
McAllister, John F.
McBride, Marshall
McCombs, Matthew
McDonell, J. C.
McDonald, John
McDonald, William
McFeely, George
Morrison, H. R.
Morrison, Joseph
Morgan, John H.
Morgan, Billingsby
Quigg, Frederick

Sheffer, David
Vance, Henry
Westerman, John
Williams, James
Coup, Williams. Wounded, July 28, 1864.

PROMOTED.

None.

KILLED.

Joseph McClenehan. At Gettysburg, Pa., July 3, 1863.
John Keifer, bugler. May 28, 1864.
Richard Lessnut. May 28, 1863.

DIED.

John F. Kennedy, sergeant. Disease, July 26, 1863.
Wilson Gault, corporal. Disease, December 7, 1863.
James Ewing. Disease, November 22, 1863.
Joseph M. Sheffer Disease, December 10, 1862.

DISCHARGED.

Joseph Wright, sergeant. Disability, June 5, 1862.
Samuel Morton, corporal. Disability, August 18, 1862.
Thomas Conner, corporal. Disability, April 11, 1863.
Samuel Brown. Disability, April 28, 1863.
Robert Cani. Disability, May 21, 1862.
John Douglass. By order, January 10, 1863.
William Ewing. Disability, April 28, 1862.
Hamilton Ingrin, Disability, April 10, 1863.
James M. G. Mouck. Disability, February 9, 1863.
Joseph M. Sample. Disability, January, 1863.
William Stewart. Disability, September 29, 1862.
Benjamin F. Shields. Disability, August 31, 1863.

TRANSFERRED.

J. F. Dodd. To Invalid Corps, 1863.
Andrew G. Happer. To Eleventh Pennsylvania Infantry.

DESERTED.

John Dimlar. October 31, 1862.
Wm. H. Meanor. October 31, 1862.
Wm. S. Wilson. October 31, 1862.

ORGANIZATION OF L COMPANY, FIRST REGIMENT PENNSYLVANIA RESERVE CAVALRY.

Company L was, originally, an old militia organization, called the Reading City Troop. It was reorganized by Captain J. C. A. Hoffeditz, from men principally of Berks county, with a few from Lancaster and Lebanon counties, and was mustered into the United States service as an independent company of cavalry, on the 30th day of July, 1861.

The company was stationed in the city of Baltimore, on duty at head-quarters Military Depot, about five months. It was attached to the First Regiment Pennsylvania Reserve Cavalry, October the 14th, 1861, and joined the regiment January the 5th, 1862, at Camp Pierpont, Va.

ENLISTED MEN OF L COMPANY.

Benj. F. Hull, orderly sergeant.
Sam'l H. Shiffert, first duty sergeant.
Wm. A. Tobias, second duty sergeant.

Joseph Buck, third duty sergeant. Prisoner, June 21, 1864.

Lewis M. Hoffeditz, fourth duty sergeant.

Peter Deisher, fifth duty sergeant.

Daniel Howder, quartermaster sergeant Prisoner, June 21, 1864.

Daniel Howder, commissary sergeant. Vet. vol., January 1, 1864.

John H. Johnson, first corporal. Vet. vol., January 1, 1864. Prisoner at Brandy Station, Va., June 9, 1863, also June 21, 1864.

Robert M. Devine, second corporal. Vet. vol., January 1, 1864.

John Kreamer, third corporal. Wounded at Culpepper, Va., September 13, 1863.

Thomas Wendling, fourth corporal. Vet. vol., February 1, 1864. Prisoner, June 21, 1864.

John M. Algaier, fifth corporal.

David Mundshower, sixth corporal.

Dewilla H. Long, seventh corporal. Vet. vol., February 1, 1864.

Francis M. Coover. Wounded at New Hope Church, Va., November 27, 1863.

Gehris, James

Buck, Peter C.

Fagan, Patrick, blacksmith.

Reber, Jacob H.

Addis, Daniel. Wounded at Brandy Station, June 9, 1863.

Billman, Samuel

Brownmiller, H. H. Vet. vol., January 1, 1864. Wounded, June 21, 1864.

Bachman, Aaron E. Prisoner at New Hope Church, November 27, 1863.

Burns, William.

Black, Hugh W. Vet. vol., January 1, 1864.

Borkman, John O.

Brown, John

Doyle, John H. Prisoner at Cedar Mountain, August 9, 1862.

Derrick, Henry. Wounded at New Hope Church, November 27, 1863.

Doyle, Jago

Fisher, Peris S.

Fresse, Geo. P.

Gehert, Hamilton

Horrock, Abraham

Moyer, Mahlon G.

Irvine, Wm. H. Vet. vol., February 1, 1864.

Irvin, Robert F. Vet. vol., January 1, 1864.

James, Geo. W. Vet. vol., January 1, 1864. Prisoner, June 21, 1864.

Knauss, Thomas. Prisoner at Cedar Mountain, August 9, 1862. Wounded at New Hope Church, November 27, 1863.

Lindenmuth, J. H. A.

Laven, Albert S.

Lindley, Thomas. Wounded at Culpepper, Va., September, 13, 1863.

Loy, Henry W. Vet. vol, February 1, 1864.

Minker, Henry

Moyer, Adam. Vet. vol., January 1, 1864.

McElwee, Andrew
Newkirk, John
Noecker, Augustus R.
Pfleager, Samuel M.
Porter, Isaac
Reed, Samuel. Vet. vol., January 1, 1864. Wounded, June 21, 1864.
Rightmeyer, Wm. H. Vet. vol., January 1, 1864.
Rogers, Joseph F.
Rudy, Henry S. Vet. vol., February 1, 1864.
Rolland, Jacob
Ruigler, Daniel S.
Stoltz, John. Vet. vol., January 1, 1864. Prisoner, June 21, 1864.
Small, Samuel. Vet. vol., January 1, 1864.
Seidens, Isaac
Vernervault, George
Wagner, Reuben
Warner, Augustus H. Vet. vol., January 1, 1864.
Werner, William W., bugler. Vet. vol., January 1, 1864.
Wilson, George P.
Winne, Barney
Zimmerman, George

RECRUITS RECEIVED FEBRUARY 28, 1864.

Gries, Charles
Hendricks, Samuel
Connard, James
Reefsnyder, David B.
Ringler, Jacob
Augstall, James

Bertelott, Mayburg
Robst, Isaac. Prisoner, June 21, 1864.
Brenizer, Franklin. Prisoner, June 21, 1864.
Bower, Thomas
Dixon, Daniel R.
Griger, David H. Prisoner, June 21, 1864.
Gross, John
Glenay, Thomas
Houston, Joseph
Jackson, Robert W.
Jackson, John
Keller, Jonas
Leiser, Wm. B. Wounded, July 28, 1864.
Reed, Daniel. Prisoner, June 25, 1864.
Sanders, James
Strasser, Jesse
Snyder, David
Sanders, Jonathan
Sanders, Geo. F.
Smith, Reuben
Lotz, Wm. D.
Herring, John
Lesher, Cyrus
Ramer, Thomas
Soheirer, Martin

PROMOTED.

Charles Lichtenthaller. Sergeant to second lieutenant, 1861.

David S. Buxton. Sergeant to second lieutenant, June 26, 1863.

George W. Fincher. Private to regimental quartermaster sergeant, November 1, 1862.

KILLED.

Michael Donovan, sergeant. At Brandy Station, Va.,
Jeremiah Gronwich. By guerrillas, Oct. 17, 1863.
John Miller. On railroad.
John Kramer. June 21, 1864.
Robert Jackson. June 21, 1864.
John Doyle. June 21, 1864.
George P. Freeze. May 21, 1864.

DIED.

John Black. Disease, April 25, 1862.
Joseph R. Lacy. Disease, December 3, 1863.
Henry Mochamer. Disease, April 7, 1862.
George Patterson. Disease, December 8, 1862.
Levi Reeder. Disease, September 10, 1862.
William Werks. Disease, December 26, 1863.
George Kemp, sergeant. Disease, July 17, 1863.

DISCHARGED.

Cyrus Bentz, sergeant. Disability, October 6, 1861.
Jeremiah K. Rhoads, sergeant. Disability, March 10, 1863.
Wm. D. Hoppenheffer, sergeant. Disability, November 8, 1861.
Augustus H. Rhoades, sergeant. Disability, March 10, 1863.
Benjamin F. Bright, sergeant. By order.
Benoval G. Pretzman, corporal. Disability, June 27, 1862.
John Giles, corporal. Disability, December 9, 1862.
Nicholas Seyfert. Disability, December 16, 1861.
Isaac S. Dissenger. Disability, November 23, 1861.

James M. Hauter, sergeant. Disability, November 3, 1862.
Charles L. Harrison. Disability, May 6, 1862.
Peter Humble. Disability, March 16, 1862.
John A. Kerns. Disability, December 8, 1862.
Lewis Kraushorf. Disability.
Peter Noll. Disability.
Samuel Ness. Disability, April 19, 1862.
Joseph Ritter. Disability, December 16, 1863.
Effinger Rhoads. Disability, December 17, 1862
Daniel H. Ruth. Disability, December 16, 1861.
Aaron Stann. Disability, November 8, 1861.
Lewis Sherman. Disability, August 11, 1861.

TRANSFERRED.

George Kester. To brigade band, November 1, 1862.
Urias Fink. To Signal Corps.
Julius Wideman. To Insane Asylum.

DESERTED.

Richard Reinholt. October 30, 1861.
Daniel Folk. November 11, 1861.
Reuben Homan. December, 1861.
John Randenbush. November 16, 1862.
Jesse Wise. July 19, 1863.

ORGANIZATION OF M COMPANY, FIRST REGIMENT PENNSYLVANIA RESERVE CAVALRY.

Company M was recruited and organized at Reading, Berks county, Pennsylvania, by Captain Thomas S. Richards; George D. Hill, first lieutenant; and

Albert Shollenberger, second lieutenant; and mustered into the United States service at Harrisburg, on the 5th day of August, 1861.

Left Harrisburg on the 6th day of August for Baltimore, and here the company was armed and equipped.

First Lieutenant, George D. Hill, resigning, George D. Leaf was appointed second lieutenant, and Albert Shollenberger, first lieutenant.

Drilling and doing orderly duty in the city, until the 3d of October, when the company was ordered to the Eastern Shore of Virginia, where, in conjunction with the Fourth Wisconsin infantry and Nim's battery, all under the command of Major-General Lockwood, was engaged in scouting and picketing, until the 24th of December, when it returned to Baltimore, and on the 7th of January, 1862, joined the First Pennsylvania Reserve Crvalry, at Camp Pierpont, Virginia.

While on duty, on the Eastern Shore, made numerous excursions down the bay, overhauling smugglers and seizing large quantities of contraband goods.

On a scout made to Pontateague Landing, (October the 9th,) the company captured seven cannon, caisons and harness; and on the 10th, at the town of Eastville, seized another cannon and about fifteen hundred (1500) stand of small arms.

ENLISTED MEN OF M COMPANY.

John Rothenberger, orderly sergeant. Vet. vol., January 1, 1864. Wounded July 12, 1864.

Wm. A. Scott, first duty sergeant. Vet. vol., February 1, 1864.

George S. Glissen, second duty sergeant. Vet. vol., February 1, 1864. Wounded May 28, 1864.

James R. Aten, third duty sergeant.

Charles B. Miller, fourth duty sergeant. Vet. vol., January 1, 1864. Wounded, August 14, 1864.

E. H. Britton, fifth duty sergeant. Wounded at New Hope Church, November 27, 1863. Vet. vol., February 1, 1864.

Henry P. Smith, quartermaster sergeant. Wounded December 12, 1862, at Fredericksburg, Va.

Frederick Munson, commissary sergeant. Wounded at Culpepper, September 13, 1863.

A. Shollenberger, first corporal. Vet. vol., February 1, 1864.

Henry F. Williams, second corporal. Prisoner, June 10, 1862. Vet. vol., February 1, 1864. Wounded, May 28, 1864.

Anthony Wolf, third corporal. Vet. vol., February 1, 1864.

Charles Morrisy, fourth corporal. Vet. vol., February 1, 1864. Prisoner, June 24, 1864.

Edward L. McGinley, fifth corporal. Vet. vol., February 1, 1864.

Shollenberger, D. B.

Confer, N. F. Wounded at Falmouth, April 19, 1862, and at Culpepper, September 13, 1863. Vet. vol., February 1, 1864.

Kline, H. B.

Carpenter, E. W.

Harper, Wm. A. Prisoner at Brandy Station, June 9, 1863.

Engle, Charles H. Prisoner at Brandy Station, June 9, 1863.

Wingard, John L. Vet. vol., February 1, 1864.

Neiman, Henry

Hawley, M. P. Vet. vol., February 1, 1864.

Hoffman, Henry. Vet. vol., February 1, 1864.

Britton, George H.

Britton, John

Brown, Samuel. Wounded, May 28, 1864.

Boyer, Thomas R.

Buckelman, Wm.

Carter, Daniel. Vet. vol., January 1, 1864.

Casper, Peter. Vet. vol., February 1, 1864.

Ebert Geo. W. Vet. vol., January 1, 1864. Wounded, May 28, 1864.

Faster, George. Prisoner, August, 1862.

Fisher, James. Vet. vol., January 1, 1864.

Feather, Jacob

Frill, Jacob

French, Oriville

Garison, John

Geltner, Charles. Prisoner, August, 1862. Vet. vol., January 1, 1864.

Griffith, William. Wounded at Falmouth, Va., April 18, 1862. Vet. vol., February 1, 1864.

Gable John P.

Harrighan, David. Wounded at Brandy Station, January 9, and at New Hope Church, Va., November 27, 1863.

Kline, George W. Vet. vol., February 1, 1864.

Leeds, William. Wounded at Brandy Station, June 9, 1863. Vet. vol., February 26, 1864.

Lindenmuth, N. Vet. vol., February 1, 1864.

Lose, Nicholas H. Vet. vol., January 1, 1864.

Martin, Thomas A. Wounded at Falmouth April 18, and at Fredericksburg, December 12, 1862.

McEwen, William

McEwen, John. Prisoner, September 6, 1862.

McGarrigal, Patrick

McGinley, Daniel. Vet. vol., Februray 1, 1864.

McGinley, John

Miller, George. Vet. vol., February 1, 1864.

Moore, Levi

Muthart, E. F. Vet. vol., January 1, 1864.

Musser, Geo. W. Vet. vol., February 1, 1864.

Miller, Don Corles

Paulis, George. Vet. vol., February 1, 1864.

Phillips, Monroe. Wounded at Culpepper, Va., September, 13, 1863.

Rapp, Henry A. Vet. vol., February 1, 1864.

Richards, Joseph. Vet. vol., January 1, 1864.

Roberts, John. Vet. vol., February 19, 1864.

Scott, Charles E. Wounded at Culpepper, Va., Sep- 13, 1863. Vet. vol., January 1, 1864.

Shealer, Augustus. Vet. vol., February 1, 1864.

Sheets, John. Prisoner, August 11, 1862. Vet. vol., January 1, 1864.

Shappell, Jeremiah. Vet. vol., February 1, 1864.

Snovel, John. Vet. vol., February 1, 1864.

Stetler, Henry. Vet. vol., February 1, 1864. Wounded, May 28, 1864.

Strine, Robert. Vet. vol., January 1, 1864.

Souder, William. Wounded at Culpepper, September 13, 1863. Vet. vol., February 14, 1863.

Urner, Henry P. Vet. vol., February 1, 1864.

Williamson, Charles. Vet. vol., February 1, 1864.

Winegardner, Lewis. Vet. vol., February 1, 1864.

Winegardner, William. Wounded at Culpepper, Va., September, 1863. Vet. vol., February 1, 1864.

Witmer, Joseph H. Vet. vol., February 1, 1864. Wounded, May 28, 1864.

Yocum, David. Prisoner, July 17, 1863.

Klinck, John

Scott, Rob't H., bugler. Recruit.

PROMOTED.

Henderson Sample. To second lieutenant, December, 1861.

J. S. Wright. Sergeant to second lieutenant, February 12, 1863.

Job H. Cole. Sergeant to battalion adjutant, March 1, 1862.

KILLED.

Patrick Devlin. At Falmouth, April 16, 1862.

Thomas Morton. At Falmouth, April 16, 1862.

Michael Rudy. At Falmouth, April 16, 1862.

DIED.

Henry F. Potter. Wounds, 1863.

Sam'l Rhoads. Wounds, November 26, 1863.

John Rodenwalt. Disease, September 23, 1863.

George Shaffer. Disease, September, 1861.

Wm. Strine. Disease, September, 1861.

A. T. Bear. Disease, August 29, 1862.
Charles Flag. Disease, August 12, 1862.

DISCHARGED.

A. S. Shollenberger, sergeant. Disability.
Barkley, M. Denny. Disability.
John Wetzel. Disability.
George Mentzer. Disability, 1861.
Henry Long Disability, September, 1861.
J. W. Cochran. Disability, September, 1861.
Jeremiah Strine. Disability, September, 1861.
Henry Strine. By order of court martial, 1861.
Thomas McGlown. Disability, October, 1861.
Thomas Devine. Disability, April 18, 1862.
J. T. Jackson. Disability, April 20, 1862.
M. M. Margnet. Disability, May 18, 1862.
W. R. Shollenberger. Disability, May 18, 1862.
Wm. Miller. Disability, June 6, 1862.
W. Montgomery. Disability, June 6, 1862.
Joseph Hale. Disability, July 5, 1862.
Patrick McNamara. Disability, July 2, 1862.
J. H. Miller. Disability, July 2, 1862.
A. B. James. Wounds, August 12, 1862.
Joel Black. Disability, March 27, 1862.
R. H. Baxter. Disability, October 20, 1862.
A. B. Kerst, sergeant. Disability, October 23, 1862.
B. P. Potts, sergeant. Disability, October 23, 1862.
Daniel Moore. Disability, October 25, 1862.
Sam'l Karver. Disability, November 26, 1862.
William Potell. Disability, Decemher 30, 1862.
James Allison. Disability, January 15, 1863.
Edward Moone. Disability, February 19, 1862.

TRANSFERRED.

Thomas Grimsley. To brigade band, January 1, 1863.

DESERTED.

Finegan Smith. September, 1861.
Henry B. Wagner. December, 1861.
Thomas D. Grimsley. September, 1861.

www.ingramcontent.com/pod-product-compliance
Lightning Source LLC
LaVergne TN
LVHW011207110826
845150LV00006B/1345